"十二五"职业教育国家规划教材
经全国职业教育教材审定委员会审定

汽车实用英语

（第二版）

马林才　主　编
王　芳　副主编
韩建保　主　审

人民交通出版社
China Communications Press

内 容 提 要

本书是"十二五"职业教育国家规划教材,是在各高等职业院校积极践行和创新先进职业教育思想和理念,深入推进"校企合作、工学结合"人才培养模式的大背景下,由交通职业教育教学指导委员会汽车运用与维修专业指导委员会根据新的教学标准和课程标准组织编写而成。

本教材共10个项目,分别选编了四冲程发动机构造与工作过程介绍、发动机燃油供给系认识、发动机冷却系和润滑系认识、汽车底盘构造认识、汽车电气设备和主动安全系统介绍、汽车车身电气设备和被动安全系统的介绍、新能源汽车介绍、汽车性能参数及检测设备介绍、汽车故障诊断仪和数据流、汽车使用说明书及维修资料等方面的汽车专业英语短文。

本书主要供高职高专院校汽车运用技术、汽车技术服务与营销、汽车电子技术、汽车整形技术和汽车检测与维修等专业的教学使用,也可作为相关行业岗位培训或自学用书,同时可供汽车维修人员学习参考。

图书在版编目(CIP)数据

汽车实用英语/马林才主编. — 2版. —北京:人民交通出版社,2014.9
"十二五"职业教育国家规划教材
ISBN 978-7-114-11239-3

Ⅰ.①汽… Ⅱ.①马… Ⅲ.①汽车工程—英语—高等职业教育—教材 Ⅳ.①H31

中国版本图书馆CIP数据核字(2014)第039257号

Qiche Shiyong Yingyu
书　　名:汽车实用英语(第二版)
著 作 者:马林才
责任编辑:翁志新　李　洁
出版发行:人民交通出版社
地　　址:(100011)北京市朝阳区安定门外外馆斜街3号
网　　址:http://www.ccpress.com.cn
销售电话:(010)59757973
总 经 销:人民交通出版社发行部
经　　销:各地新华书店
印　　刷:北京市密东印刷有限公司
开　　本:787×1092　1/16
印　　张:11
字　　数:248千
版　　次:2012年6月　第1版
　　　　　2014年9月　第2版
印　　次:2018年8月　第4次印刷　累计第6次印刷
书　　号:ISBN 978-7-114-11239-3
定　　价:38.00元

(有印刷、装订质量问题的图书由本社负责调换)

交通职业教育教学指导委员会
汽车运用与维修专业指导委员会

主 任 委 员： 魏庆曜

副主任委员： 张尔利　汤定国　马伯夷

委　　　员： 王凯明　王晋文　刘　锐　刘振楼　刘越琪
　　　　　　　许立新　吴宗保　张京伟　李富仓　杨维和
　　　　　　　陈文华　陈贞健　周建平　周柄权　金朝勇
　　　　　　　唐　好　屠卫星　崔选盟　黄晓敏　彭运钧
　　　　　　　舒　展　韩　梅　解福泉　詹红红　裴志浩
　　　　　　　魏俊强　魏荣庆

秘　　　书： 秦兴顺

编审委员会
Editorial Committee

公共平台组
组　　长：魏庆曜
副 组 长：崔选盟　周林福
成　　员：王福忠　林　松　李永芳　叶　钢　刘建伟　郭　玲
　　　　　马林才　黄志杰　边　伟　屠卫星　孙　伟
特邀主审：郭远辉　杨启勇　崔振民　韩建保　李　朋　陈德阳

机电维修专门化组
组　　长：汤定国
副 组 长：陈文华　杨　洸
成　　员：吕　坚　彭小红　陈　清　杨宏进　刘振楼　王保新
　　　　　秦兴顺　刘　成　宋保林　张杰飞
特邀主审：卞良勇　黄俊平　寒小平　张西振　疏祥林　李　全
　　　　　黄晓敏　周建平

维修服务顾问专门化组
组　　长：杨维和
副 组 长：刘　焰　杨宏进
成　　员：韦　峰　罗　双　周　勇　钱锦武　陈文均　刘资媛
　　　　　金加龙　王彦峰　杨柳青
特邀主审：吴玉基　刘　锐　张　俊　邹小明　熊建国

保险与公估专门化组
组　　长：张尔利
副 组 长：阳小良　彭朝晖
成　　员：李远军　陈建宏　侯晓民　肖文光　曹云刚　廖　明
　　　　　荆叶平　彭晓艳
特邀主审：文爱民　任成尧　李富仓　刘　璘　冷元良

第二版前言
Preface

根据教育部的《关于"十二五"职业教育国家规划教材选题立项的函》（教职成司函[2013]184号）的通知精神，人民交通出版社出版的教材《汽车实用英语》符合"十二五"职业教育国家规划教材选题立项要求。

2013年10月，人民交通出版社组织十几所院校的汽车专业教师代表，在青岛召开了"十二五"职业教育国家规划教材汽车类专业立项教材修订会议。会议根据《教育部关于"十二五"职业教育教材建设的若干意见》（教职成[2012]9号）文件精神，经过认真研究讨论，吸收了教材使用院校教师的意见和建议，确定了立项教材的修订方案。

本书是在第一版的基础上，在会议确定的修订方案指导下完成的，教材的内容修订主要体现在以下几个方面：删掉过时的内容，如与化油器相关的部分内容；增加熔断丝盒内部各种熔断丝的英文含义；增加故障诊断仪中常出现的故障描述短句；修改第一版中的图片文字或音标出现的错误。

本教材的修订工作，具体分工如下：

本教材由浙江交通职业技术学院马林才教授担任主编，浙江交通职业技术学院王芳副教授担任副主编，北京理工大学韩建保教授担任主审。其中，浙江交通职业技术学院马林才教授负责修订项目1、项目2和项目3；杭州长运运输集团有限公司金柏正教授级高级工程师负责修订项目4；浙江交通职业技术学院鲍婷婷讲师负责修订项目5和项目6；浙江交通职业技术学院刘大学讲师负责修订项目7和项目8；浙江交通职业技术学院王芳副教授负责修订项目9和项目10。

限于编者水平，书中难免有疏漏和错误之处，恳请广大读者提出宝贵建议，以便进一步修改和完善。

编者
2014年1月

前 言
Preface

为落实《国家中长期教育改革和发展规划纲要（2010—2020年）》精神，深化职业教育教学改革，积极推进课程改革和教材建设，满足职业教育发展的新需求，交通职业教育教学指导委员会汽车运用与维修专业指导委员会按照工学结合一体化课程的开发程序和方法编制完成了《汽车运用技术专业教学标准与课程标准》，在此基础上组织全国交通职业技术院校汽车运用技术专业的骨干教师及相关企业的专业技术人员，编写了本套规划教材，供高职高专院校汽车运用技术、汽车检测与维修专业教学使用。

本套教材在启动之初，交通职业教育教学指导委员会汽车运用与维修专业指导委员会又邀请了国内著名职业教育专家赵志群教授为主编人员进行了关于课程开发方法的系统培训。初稿完成后，根据课程的特点，分别邀请了企业专家、本科院校的教授和高职院校的教师进行了审阅，之后又专门召开了两次审稿会，对稿件进行了集中审定后才定稿，实现了对稿件的全过程监控和严格把关。

本套教材在编写过程中，主要编写人员认真总结了全国交通职业院校多年来的教学成果，结合了企业职业岗位的客观需求，吸收了发达国家先进的职业教育理念，教材成稿后，形成了以下特色：

1. 强调"校企合作、工学结合"

汽车运用技术专业建设，从市场调研、职业分析，到教学标准、课程标准开发，再到教材编写的全过程，都是职业院校的教师与相关企业的专业人员一起合作完成的，真正实现了学校和企业的紧密结合。本专业核心课程采用学习领域的课程模式，基于职业典型工作任务进行课程内容选择和组织，体现了工学结合的本质特征——"学习的内容是工作，通过工作实现学习"，突出学生的综合职业能力培养。

2. 强调"课程体系创新，编写模式创新"

按照整体化的职业资格分析方法，通过召开来自企业一线的实践专家研讨会分析得出职业典型工作任务，在专业教师和行业专家、教育专家共同努力下进行教学分析和设计，形成了汽车运用技术专业新的课程体系。本套教材的编写，打破了传统教材的章节体例，以具有代表性的工作任务为一个相对完整的学习过程，围绕工作任务聚焦知识和技能，体现行动导向的教学观，提升学生学习的主动性和成就感。

《汽车实用英语》是本套教材中的一本知识型学科教材，具有以下特点：

（1）采用项目引导、任务驱动的模式，符合职业教育"校企合作、工学结合"的理念。

（2）内容主要取自英文原著，涉及面广，涵盖汽车结构、汽车检测、汽车维修、汽车新技术等方面。

（3）力求简单易懂，以简单实用为目标，强调专业词汇的运用，体现高职特色。

（4）插图丰富、清晰精致、形象生动，有利于激发学生的学习兴趣。

本教材由浙江交通职业技术学院马林才副教授担任主编，广西交通职业技术学院黄志杰讲师、浙江交通职业技术学院刘大学讲师和王芳讲师担任副主编，北京理工大学韩建保教授担任主审。其中，浙江交通职业技术学院马林才副教授负责编写项目1、项目2和项目3；杭州长运运输集团有限公司金柏正高级工程师负责编写项目4；广西交通职业技术学院黄志杰讲师负责编写项目5；浙江交通职业技术学院鲍婷婷讲师负责编写项目6；浙江交通职业技术学院刘大学讲师负责编写项目7和项目8；浙江交通职业技术学院王芳讲师负责编写项目9和项目10。

限于编者经历和水平，教材内容难以覆盖全国各地的实际情况，希望各教学单位在积极选用和推广本系列教材的同时，注重总结经验，及时提出修改意见和建议，以便再版修订时补充完善。

交通职业教育教学指导委员会
汽车运用与维修专业指导委员会
2011年6月

目 录
Contents

项目1 四冲程发动机构造与工作过程介绍 ·· 1
Project 1　Introduction to the Construction and Operation
　　　　　　of a Four-stroke Engine ·· 2
　　Practical Reading　2ZZ-GE Engine ·· 12

项目2 发动机燃油供给系认识 ·· 15
Project 2　Acquaintance with Engine Fuel System ················· 16
　　Practical Reading　Engine Measurement and Performance
　　　　　　　　　　　Characteristics ·· 26

项目3 发动机冷却系和润滑系认识 ·· 29
Project 3　Acquaintance with Engine Cooling
　　　　　　and Lubricating System ·· 30
　　Practical Reading　Cooling-system Problems ················· 39

项目4 汽车底盘构造认识 ·· 42
Project 4　Acquaintance with Automotive Chassis
　　　　　　Construction ·· 43
　　Practical Reading　The Introduction of Electronically
　　Controlled Air Suspension ·· 58

项目5 汽车电气设备和主动安全系统介绍 ·· 61
Project 5　Introduction to the Automotive Electric System
　　　　　　and Active Safety Systems ·· 62
　　Practical Reading　Anti-Lock Brake System Types ················· 74

项目6 汽车车身电气设备和被动安全系统的介绍 ···································· 77
Project 6　Introduction to Automotive Body Electrical
　　　　　　Equipment and Passive Safety Systems ················· 78
　　Practical Reading　Body Electronic Module (BEM):
　　　　　　　　　　　Overview ·· 86

项目7　新能源汽车介绍 ··· 89
　　Project 7　Introduction to the New Energy Vehicles ············ 90
　　Practical Reading　New-Energy Car Strategy Proposed ·········· 98

项目8　汽车性能参数及检测设备介绍 ································· 101
　　Project 8　Introduction to Automotive Performance
　　　　　　　Parameters and Testing Equipments ················· 102
　　Practical Reading　Engine Noise Diagnosis ······················ 115

项目9　汽车故障诊断仪和数据流 ······································ 118
　　Project 9　Introduction to the Diagnostic Tester and Data
　　　　　　　Flow ·· 119
　　Practical Reading　Passat K Line Fault Diagnosis Cases ········ 129

项目10　汽车使用说明书及维修资料 ································· 131
　　Project 10　Car Manual and Maintenance Information ··········· 132
　　Practical Reading　Idle Control System rpm Lower than
　　　　　　　　　　Expected ··· 151

参考答案 ··· 154
　　项目1 ··· 154
　　项目2 ··· 155
　　项目3 ··· 156
　　项目4 ··· 157
　　项目5 ··· 158
　　项目6 ··· 159
　　项目7 ··· 160
　　项目8 ··· 161
　　项目9 ··· 162
　　项目10 ··· 163

项目1　四冲程发动机构造与工作过程介绍

学习目标

1. 认识关于四冲程发动机构造、工作过程的英语术语和词汇；
2. 理解发动机中零部件及工作过程的固定表达方法；
3. 运用所学知识，借助专业词典，对发动机各总成资料进行中英互译；
4. 在教师指导下，完成与发动机构造及工作过程相关的英语资料阅读和翻译工作；
5. 正确完成课后练习。

学习时间

4学时

任务描述

以四冲程发动机为例，学习有关发动机构造及工作过程等知识，如汽缸体、汽缸盖、活塞、连杆、进气行程、压缩行程、做功行程及排气行程等，完成相关词汇、特殊语句的认识。通过完成该任务，能阅读关于发动机构造及工作过程的外文文献，并能运用所学项目知识和翻译技巧，翻译相关文献。

引导问题

你知道下图中的英文代表什么意思吗？

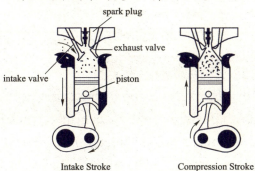

学习引导

本项目的学习，应沿着以下脉络进行：
通读全文→学习单词和语法→完成课后练习→分组讨论→课后阅读

Project 1　Introduction to the Construction and Operation of a Four-stroke Engine

introduction [,intrə'dʌkʃən]
　　　n.介绍，传入，导言，绪论，入门
stroke [strəuk]　　　　n.冲程，行程
engine ['endʒin]　　　　n.发动机
assembly [ə'sembli]
　　　n.总成，装配，部件，装置，组合体
power ['pauə]　　　n.动力，功率，能量
torque [tɔ:k]　　　n.转矩，力矩，扭矩
vehicle ['vi:ikl]　　　n.交通工具，车辆
motor ['məutə]　　　n.发动机，汽车
combustion [kəm'bʌstʃən]　　n.燃烧
electric [i'lektrik]
　　　adj.电的，电动的，充电的，能发电的
hybrid ['haibrid]　adj.混合的，混合而成的
burn [bə:n]　　　　　　　vi., vt.燃烧
petrol ['petrəl]
　　　n.[英]汽油（=[美]gasoline），挥发油
distributor [dis'tribjutə]　　　n.分电器
battery ['bætəri]　　　　　n.蓄电池
component [kəm'pəunənt]
　　　　　n.部分，部件，零件，元件
ignition [ig'niʃən]　　n.点火，点燃
lubrication [lu:bri'keiʃən]　　n.润滑油
cylinder ['silində]　n.汽缸，圆筒，圆柱体
camshaft ['kæmʃɑ:ft]　　　n.凸轮轴
intake ['inteik]　　　　n.入口，进口
spring [spriŋ]　　　　　　n.弹簧
piston ['pistən]　　　　　n.活塞
crankshaft ['kræŋkʃɑ:ft]　　n.曲轴
flywheel ['flaiwi:l]　　　　n.飞轮
starter ['stɑ:tə]　　　　　n.起动机
gear [giə]　　　n.齿轮，传动装置
bearing ['bɛəriŋ]　　　　n.轴承

The Engine Assembly

The engine is the source of power that provides the torque or turning force which is used to drive the vehicle. Engines in motor vehicles can be internal combustion, electric or a combination of the two (known as "hybrid").[1] Internal combustion engines burn the fuel inside the engine using petrol, distillate or gas. Electric motors use electricity supplied from storage batteries fitted to the vehicle. The batteries can be charged using an internal combustion engine, fuel cell, solar cell, power regeneration and external charging.[2]

The engine assembly includes the engine itself as well as all the components and systems needed to make it start and run. These include the starting, charging, cooling, ignition, lubricating, fuel and the exhaust systems. Figure 1-1 shows the basic construction of a four-cylinder engine.

Engine Construction

Components at the top of the engine are: timing belt, camshaft timing pulley, camshaft, rocker arms and shafts, intake valves and springs, exhaust valves and springs, piston (shown as Figure 1-2).

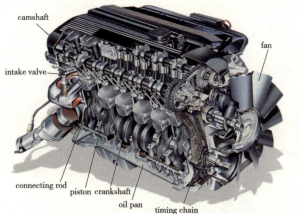
Figure 1-1 Basic construction of a four-cylinder engine

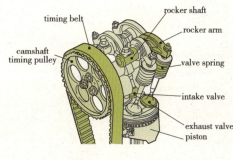
Figure 1-2 Components at the top of an engine

Components at the front of the engine are: piston, connecting rod, crankshaft, crankshaft timing pulley, timing belt, crankshaft pulley and balancer （shown as Figure 1-3）.

Components at the rear of the engine are: flywheel, starter ring gear, piston and connecting rod （shown as Figure 1-4）.

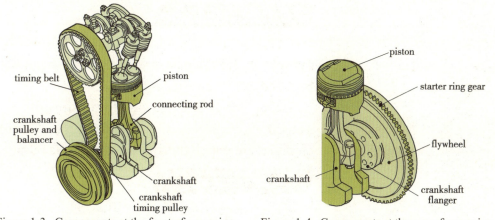

Figure 1-3 Components at the front of an engine

Figure 1-4 Components at the rear of an engine

Components at the bottom of the engine are: four pistons, connecting rods, crankshaft, crankshaft balance weights, crankshaft main-bearing journals, pulley and balancer （shown as Figure 1-5）.

Cylinder Block

The cylinder block is the largest part of the engine. It has cylinders in which the pistons operate and bearings which carry the crankshaft. In some engines, the cylinder block also carries the camshaft. The cylinders and pistons are in the upper

Word List

crankcase ['kræŋkkeis]	n. 曲轴箱
bolt [bəult]	n. 螺栓，v. 用螺栓紧固
gasket ['gæskit]	n. 汽缸垫, 衬垫
seal [si:l]	n. 封条，密封
aluminum [ə'lu:mɪnəm]	n. 铝
manifold ['mænɪfəuld]	n.（进、排气）歧管
fan [fæn]	n. 扇子，鼓风机，风扇
radiator ['reidɪeitə]	n. 散热器
coolant ['ku:lənt]	n. 冷却液

part of the cylinder block and the crankshaft is in the lower part. This lower part is called the crankcase. It has webs which carry the crankshaft main bearings.

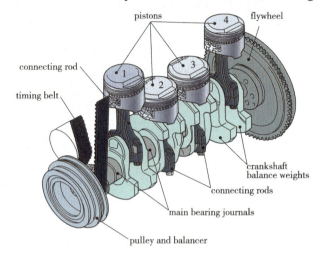

Figure 1-5　Components at the bottom of an engine

Cylinder Head

The cylinder head is bolted to the top of the cylinder block. A gasket, the cylinder-head gasket, is fitted between the parts to provide a seal. The cylinder head is made of aluminum alloy. It is shaped above each cylinder to form the combustion chambers in which the air-fuel mixture is burnt.

Valve Cover

The valve cover fits on top of the cylinder head and covers the valve mechanism. The valve cover is of aluminum alloy. A gasket is fitted between it and the top of the cylinder head to provide an oil seal.

Oil Pan

The oil pan, or sump, is attached to the bottom of the crankcase and closes off the internal parts （shown as Figure 1-6）. It also acts as a reservoir for the engine oil.

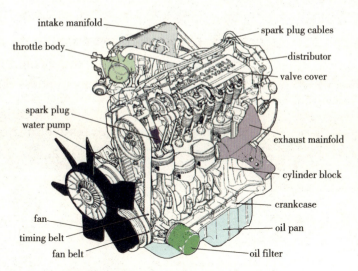

Figure 1-6 External components of an engine

🔍 Oil Pump and Oil Filter

The oil leaving the oil pump passes through the oil filter before it is circulated through the engine. The filter removes particles of carbon or other foreign material from the oil.

🔍 Intake Manifold and Exhaust Manifold

The intake manifold carries the air-fuel mixture into the engine. The exhaust manifold is on the opposite side of the engine to the intake manifold.

🔍 Fan

The fan at the front of the engine provides a flow of air through the radiator as part of the engine's cooling system.

🔍 Water Pump

The water pump is driven by the fan belt from the crankshaft pulley. It circulates coolant throughout the engine and radiator assembly.

🔍 Crankshaft and Bearings

The crankshaft is fitted to the engine block. It is supported by the main bearings to take the radial loads from the connecting rods.

🔍 Piston and Connecting Rod Assembly

The large end of the connecting rod connects to the crankshaft and the small end

Word List

arrangement [əˈreɪndʒmənt]　n.排列，安排
flange [flændʒ]　n.突缘，边缘，轮缘
function [ˈfʌŋkʃən]　n.功能，作用
distillate [ˈdɪstɪleɪt]　n.馏分油，柴油
spark [spɑːk]　n.火花
compress [kəmˈpres]　vt.压缩，浓缩
draw [drɔː]　vt.吸引，吸入
port [pɔːt]　n.通道，港口，端口
vaporize [ˈveɪpəraɪz]　vt., vi.蒸发，使蒸发
charge [tʃɑːdʒ]　n.充量，装料

connects to the piston（shown as Figure 1-7）.[3] The piston pin connects the piston to the connecting rod. The piston is fitted with three piston rings. The top two rings seal the piston to the cylinder wall and prevent combustion gases from entering the crankcase. The bottom ring prevents excessive oil from entering the combustion chamber from the crankcase.

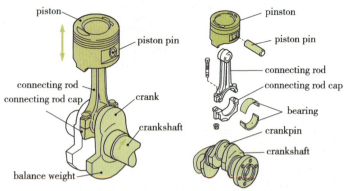

Figure 1-7　Arrangement of a piston, connecting rod and crankshaft

Flywheel

The flywheel is bolted to the flange on the rear end of the crankshaft. Its function is to keep the engine running smoothly between power strokes（shown as Figure 1-8）.

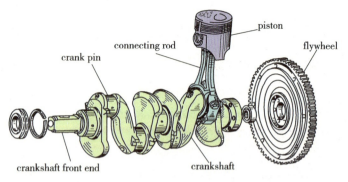

Figure 1-8　Crankshaft, flywheel and piston

Distributor, Cables and Spark Plugs

The distributor is at the rear of the cylinder

head and is driven by the camshaft. It distributes high voltage to each spark plug at the right time. This provides the spark which ignites the air-fuel mixture. The firing order for a four-cylinder engine is 1-3-4-2 or 1-2-4-3.[4] This is the sequence in which the pistons deliver the power strokes.

Camshaft

In overhead-valve engines, the camshaft is located in bearings in the cylinder block or crankcase. It is driven from the crankshaft at half the engine speed. As the cams rotate, they move the valve lifters up and down and this movement is transferred through the other parts of the valve train to the valves in the cylinder head.

Operation of the Four-stroke Engine

The most common engine is the four-stroke piston engine. These four strokes are intake stroke, compression stroke, power stroke and exhaust stroke (shown as Figure 1-9).

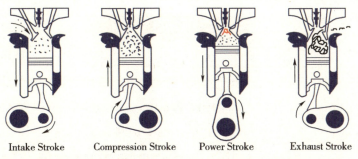

Figure 1-9 The four-stroke cycle of a petrol engine

Intake Stroke

The intake stroke commences at top dead centre (TDC) with the intake valve open and the exhaust valve closed. The piston moves downwards to draw a charge of air-fuel mixture into the cylinder through the open intake port. The mixture of air and vaporized fuel is provided by the fuel injection system.

Compression Stroke

When the piston reaches bottom dead centre (BDC) and begins to move upwards on the compression stroke, the intake valve closes. The exhaust valve is already closed, so that the air-fuel charge is compressed as the piston moves up the

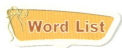

expand [ɪk'spænd]
　　　　　　　　vt.使膨胀，扩张
crankpin ['kræŋkpɪn]
　　　　　　　　n.曲柄销，连杆轴颈
automobile ['ɔːtəməbɪːl]　n.汽车
medium ['mɪːdɪəm]　n.媒体，媒介，介质

cylinder. By the time the piston reaches TDC, the mixture will be compressed to about one-eighth of its original volume. The pressure in the cylinder will also have increased.

Power Stroke

Both valves remain closed during the power stroke. As the piston reaches TDC at the end of the compression stroke, the ignition system produces a spark at the spark plug. The spark ignites the air-fuel mixture, which burns very rapidly to produce gases at high pressure in the cylinder. The expanding gases force the piston down the cylinder. The force is transferred through the connecting rod to the crankpin, causing the crankshaft to rotate.

Exhaust Stroke

As the piston again reaches BDC, the exhaust valve opens, but the intake valve remains closed. The piston moves upwards on the exhaust stroke to force the burnt gases out of the cylinder through the exhaust port. When the piston reaches TDC, the exhaust stroke is completed and so is the cycle.

Engine Classification

For identification purposes, manufacturers classify automobile engines by their cylinder arrangement, valve arrangement and type of system used to cool the engine.[5] Engine manufacturers basically use three distinct ways to arrange the cylinders in an engine: in-line, V-shape or opposed （shown as Figure 1-10）.

Manufacturers also classify engines as being either air-cooled or water-cooled. In air-cooled engines, cylinders are cooled by the air flowing around. A Water-cooled engine uses a liquid coolant as the medium to remove heat from the engine.

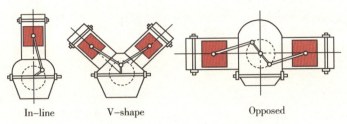

Figure 1-10　Engine configurations

Proper Names

1. solar cell　　　　　　　　　　　太阳能电池
2. fuel cell　　　　　　　　　　　　燃料电池
3. valve cover　　　　　　　　　　 气门室罩
4. aluminum alloy　　　　　　　　 铝合金
5. timing belt　　　　　　　　　　 正时皮带
6. fuel injection system　　　　　　燃油喷射系统
7. engine classification　　　　　　发动机分类
8. water pump　　　　　　　　　　水泵
9. oil pan　　　　　　　　　　　　油底壳
10. fan pulley　　　　　　　　　　 风扇皮带轮
11. piston ring　　　　　　　　　　活塞环
12. oil pump　　　　　　　　　　　机油泵
13. oil filter　　　　　　　　　　　机油滤清器
14. ignition distributor　　　　　　 点火分电器
15. rocker arm　　　　　　　　　　（气门）摇臂
16. internal combustion engine　　　内燃机
17. air-fuel mixture　　　　　　　　空气燃油混合物（可燃混合气）
18. intake stroke　　　　　　　　　进气行程
19. compression stroke　　　　　　 压缩行程
20. power stroke　　　　　　　　　做功行程
21. exhaust stroke　　　　　　　　 排气行程
22. top dead centre（TDC）　　　　 上止点
23. connecting rod　　　　　　　　 连杆
24. intake valve　　　　　　　　　 进气门

25. intake manifold 进气歧管
26. exhaust valve 排气门
27. bottom dead centre（BDC） 下止点
28. spark plug 火花塞
29. combustion chamber 燃烧室
30. cylinder head 汽缸盖
31. cylinder block 汽缸体
32. main bearing journal 主轴承轴颈
33. pulley and balancer 皮带轮和平衡重
34. radial load 径向荷载
35. ring gear 齿圈

Notes

[1] Engines in motor vehicles can be internal combustion, electric or a combination of the two（known as "hybrid"）.

翻译：机动车的动力装置可以是内燃机、电动机或者两者的组合（如所谓的"混合动力"）。

语法：known as 译为"称为，被认为"。

[2] The batteries can be charged using an internal combustion engine, fuel cell, solar cell, power regeneration and external charging.

翻译：蓄电池可以用内燃机、燃料电池、太阳能电池、再生能量或外部电源进行充电。

[3] The large end of the connecting rod connects to the crankshaft and the small end connects to the piston.

翻译：连杆大端连接到曲轴，连杆小端连接到活塞。

[4] The firing order for a four-cylinder engine is 1-3-4-2 or 1-2-4-3.

翻译：4缸发动机的点火顺序为1-3-4-2或1-2-4-3。

[5] For identification purposes, manufacturers classify automobile engines by their cylinder arrangement, valve arrangement and type of system used to cool the engine.

翻译：发动机制造商将汽车发动机按汽缸排列形式、气门布置形式以及冷却系统的类型进行分类。

语法：for identification purposes 作目的状语。

Exercises

1. Choose the best answer from the following choices according to the text.

1）The_____ is the source of power that provides the torque or turning force which is used to drive the vehicle.

  A. engine   B. cylinder   C. bore   D. crankshaft

2）The cylinders and pistons are in the _____ the cylinder block and the crankshaft is in the lower part.

  A. left part of   B. upper part of   C. right part of   D. bottom part of

3）The _____ ignites the air-fuel mixture, which burns very rapidly to produce gases at high pressure in the cylinder.

  A. distributor   B. camshaft   C. spark   D. engine

4）Flywheel inertia tends to keep the _____ rotating at a constant speed.

  A. crankshaft   B. camshaft   C. connecting rod   D. piston

2. Translate the following words or phrases into Chinese.

1）intake stroke   2）timing gear   3）water pump
4）connecting rod   5）combustion chamber   6）crankpin
7）bottom dead centre   8）cylinder head   9）fan pulley

3. Translate the following words or phrases into English.

1）汽缸体   2）太阳能电池   3）曲轴箱
4）油底壳   5）正时皮带   6）活塞环
7）点火分电器   8）火花塞   9）主轴承轴颈

4. Translate the following sentences into Chinese.

1）These include the starting, charging, cooling, ignition, lubricating, fuel and the exhaust systems.

2）These four strokes are intake stroke, compression stroke, power stroke and exhaust stroke.

3）The force is transferred through the connecting rod to the crankpin, causing the crankshaft to rotate.

5. Translate the words or phrases in the following figure into Chinese.

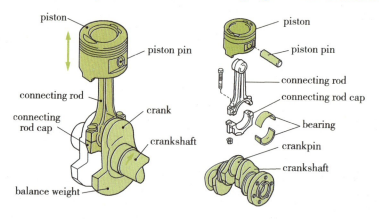

Practical Reading　　2ZZ–GE Engine

The 2ZZ-GE engine is an in-line, 4-cylinder, 1.8-liter, 16-valve DOHC engine （shown as Figure 1-11）.[1] This engine meets the European STEP Ⅲ regulations.

The VVTL-i system （Variable Valve Timing and Lift-intelligent） system, the DIS （Direct Ignition System） and an air injection system have been adopted on this engine in order to improve performance, fuel economy and reduce exhaust emissions.[2]

Word List

regulation [regju'leɪʃ(ə)n]　n.规则，规章
layout ['leɪaʊt]　n.设计，布置，版面安排

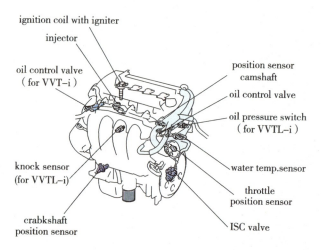

Figure 1-11　Layout of engine's main components

Proper Names

1. engine component　　　　发动机零部件
2. fuel economy　　　　　　燃油经济性
3. DOHC　　　　　　　　　双顶置凸轮轴
4. VVTL-i　　　　　　　　 智能气门升程和可变气门正时
5. DIS　　　　　　　　　　直接点火系统

 Notes

[1] The 2ZZ-GE engine is an in-line, 4-cylinder, 1.8-liter, 16-valve DOHC engine.

翻译：2ZZ-GE发动机是直列、4缸、1.8升排量、16气门、双顶置凸轮轴发动机。

[2] The VVTL-i system (Variable Valve Timing and Lift-intelligent) system, the DIS (Direct Ignition System) and an air injection system have been adopted on this engine in order to improve performance, fuel economy and reduce exhaust emissions.

翻译：为提高发动机动力性，燃油经济性及降低排放，本发动机采用了VVTL-i（可变气门正时—智能气门升程系统）、DIS（直接点火系统）、空气喷射系统。

 学习资料

相关链接及网址：
[1] http://www.a-car.com
[2] http://www.ntis.gov.au/Default.aspx?/trainingpackage/AUR05
[3] http://www.ford.com/

推荐书目

[1] 王怡民.汽车专业英语[M].北京：人民交通出版社，2003.
[2] 马林才.汽车实用英语（下）[M].北京：人民交通出版社，2005.

[3] 陈文华. 汽车发动机构造与维修[M].北京：北京航空航天大学出版社，2007.

[4] William K.Toboldt, & Larry Johnson. Automotive Encyclopedia[M]. South Holland, Illinois: The Goodheart-willcox Company, Inc，1983.

项目2　发动机燃油供给系认识

学习目标

1. 认识关于燃油供给系的组成和作用等的英语术语和词汇；
2. 理解电子燃油喷射系统的固定表达方法；
3. 运用所学知识，借助专业词典，对关于燃油供给系资料进行中英互译；
4. 在教师指导下，完成与发动机燃油供给系相关的英语资料阅读和翻译工作；
5. 正确完成课后练习。

学习时间

4学时

任务描述

以汽油发动机为例，学习有关发动机燃油供给系知识，油箱、油泵、燃油滤清器、供油管、喷油器、燃油压力调节器及回油管以及电子燃油喷射系统等，完成相关词汇、特殊语句的认识。通过完成该任务，能阅读关于发动机的燃油供给系的外文文献，并能运用所学项目知识和翻译技巧，翻译相关文献。

引导问题

你知道下图中的英文代表什么意思吗？

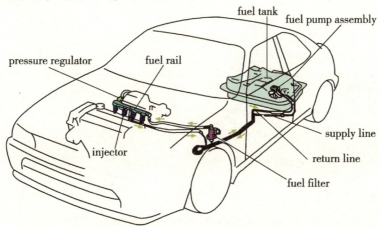

学习引导

本项目的学习，应沿着以下脉络进行：

通读全文→学习单词和语法→完成课后练习→分组讨论→课后阅读

Project 2　Acquaintance with Engine Fuel System

Introduction

The fuel system has the job of supplying a combustible mixture of air and fuel to the engine. There are two different types of petrol fuel systems: systems with a carburetor and systems with electronic fuel injection （EFI）. Carburetor fuel systems and EFI systems are designed to deliver the fuel mixture to the engine in a combustible form, but each system does it in a different way.[1] One basic difference is that carburetors atomize the fuel, and injectors spray the fuel.

Electronic Fuel Injection System

EFI systems use injectors to spray the fuel. There are two different systems: multipoint injection and throttle body injection （also called single-point injection）. In both systems, the injectors are electronically controlled. Multipoint injection is the most commonly used, and consists of fuel tank, fuel pump, filter, fuel rail, injectors, pressure regulator, air cleaner and ducting, throttle body, airflow meter, plenum chamber, intake manifold and electronic control unit （ECU）（shown as Figure 2-1）. An EFI

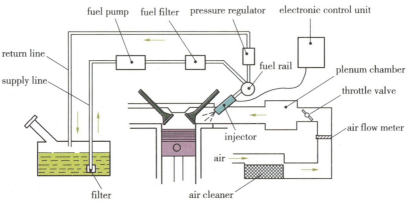

Figure 2-1　Arrangement of a basic EFI system

system can be considered as having three subsystems, each of which has a number of components. These subsystems are: fuel supply system, air intake system and electronic control system.

Fuel Supply System

The fuel supply system consists of the fuel tank, fuel pump, fuel filter, fuel supply pipe, fuel injector, fuel pressure regulator, and fuel return pipe (shown as Figure 2-2).[2] Fuel is delivered from the tank to the injector by means of an electric fuel pump. Contaminants are filtered out by a high capacity in line fuel filter. Fuel is maintained at a constant pressure by means of a fuel pressure regulator. Any fuel that is not delivered to the intake manifold by the injector is returned to the tank through a fuel return pipe. The injectors are connected into the fuel rail and spray fuel directly into the intake ports of the engine. The amount of fuel delivered by the injectors and their timing are controlled by the electronic control unit (ECU). During cold engines starting, many engines incorporate a cold start injector designed to improve startability below a specified coolant temperature (shown as Figure 2-3).

diaphragm ['daiəfræm]	n.隔板，膜片
eccentric [ik'sentrik]	n.偏心部分，偏心轮
subsystem ['sʌbsistəm]	n.子系统，分系统
contaminant [kən'tæmɪnənt]	n.致污物，污染物
incorporate [ɪn'kɔːpəreit]	vi.合并，混合
startability [staːtə'bɪlɪtɪ]	n.起动性
induction [ɪn'dʌkʃən]	n.吸入，进气

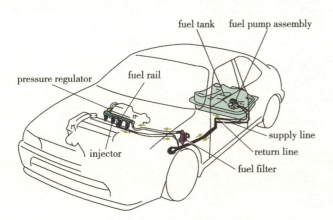

Figure 2-2 Main parts of an EFI fuel supply system

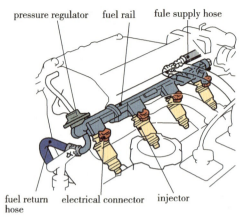

Figure 2-3　Fuel rail and injectors for a four-cylinder engine

🔍 Fuel Tank and Fuel Lines

There are three pipes（or lines） between the fuel tank at the rear of the vehicle and the components in the engine compartment.[3] There are also pipes or hoses between some components and the engine. The pipes connected to the fuel tank are: the fuel supply line, the return line, the vapor line and other lines. The fuel supply line is used to carry fuel from the tank to the filter and then to the fuel pump. The return line returns surplus fuel from the pump. The vapor line vents the fuel tank to the charcoal canister. Other lines connect the fuel pump to the carburetor, and the charcoal canister to the engine （shown as Figure 2-4）.

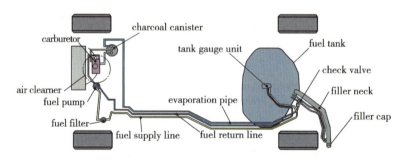

Figure 2-4　Main components of a carburetor fuel system

🔍 Fuel Filters

A fine gauze filter is fitted to the suction pipe in the fuel tank, and a line filter is fitted in the supply line between the fuel tank and the fuel pump, or between the fuel pump and the carburetor.[4] The filter traps dirt and water that may have entered the fuel tank.

Fuel Pumps

A simplified mechanical fuel pump has an inlet and an outlet valve and a flexible diaphragm which is moved up and down by the action of the rocker arm. The end of the rocker arm is operated by an eccentric on the camshaft.

The Air Induction System

The purpose of the air induction system is to filter, meter, and measure intake air flow into the engine. The air induction system consists of the air cleaner, air flow meter, throttle valve, air intake chamber, intake manifold runner, and intake valve (shown as Figure 2-5).[5]

combustible [kəmˈbʌstɪbəl]	adj.易燃的，可燃的
carburetor [kɑːbjuˈetə]	n.化油器，汽化器
injection [ɪnˈdʒekʃən]	n.注射，喷射
deliver[diˈlivə]	vt.递送，提供，释放，移交
atomize [ˈætəmaɪz]	vt.使雾化
injector[ɪnˈdʒektə]	n.喷油器，喷嘴
spray[spreɪ]	vt.,vi.喷雾，喷洒
conventional [kənˈvenʃənəl]	adj.常规的，传统的
pipe[paɪp]	n.管子，管道
hose [həuz]	n.软管，胶皮管
vapor[ˈveɪpə]	n.蒸汽
surplus[ˈsəːpləs]	adj.过剩的，多余的
vent[vent]	vt.放出，排除，给…开孔
gauze[gɔːz]	n.丝网，薄纱，网纱，沙罗
trap[træp]	vt.诱捕，困住
sensor [ˈsensə]	n.传感器
wiring [ˈwaɪərɪŋ]	n.配线
nozzle [ˈnɔzəl]	n.管口，喷嘴
droplet [ˈdrɔplɪt]	n.小滴

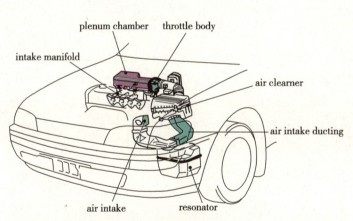

Figure 2-5 Air intake system for an EFI engine

Electronic Control System

The electronic control system consists of various engine sensors, Electronic Control Unit (ECU), fuel injector assemblies, and related wiring. It can receive information, inputs and send signals to other components, outputs. Its main function in the fuel system is to tell the injectors when they should spray and how long they should remain open. The length of time that the injectors are open determines the amount of fuel that is sprayed into the engine. The ECU receives signals from the various sensors, processes them and adjusts the amount of fuel that is delivered from the injectors. This enables the air-fuel ratio to be adjusted to suit many different operating conditions（shown as Figure 2-6）.

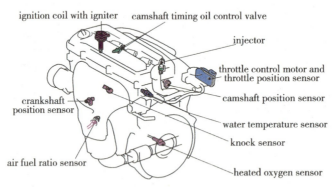

Figure 2-6　Main components of an electronic control system

Single Point Fuel Injection and Multipoint Fuel Injection

In the EFI system, it is possible to have systems using only one injector per engine（single point fuel injection）or one injector per cylinder（multipoint fuel injection）.[6] In the single point fuel injection system, it combines a single（or twin）fuel injection nozzle, fuel pressure regulator, throttle valve, throttle switch and idle speed regulator into a compact throttle body unit. This unit is mounted directly on the intake manifold, in a similar manner to a conventional carburetor. This type of EFI system is more commonly called Throttle Body Fuel Injection. Fuel is injected into the area around the throttle valve, where air velocity is at a maximum; thus ensuring fuel droplets are thoroughly atomized and will be distributed throughout the air mass. While in multipoint fuel injection system, injectors deliver fuel directly onto the closed, but hot, intake valve of each cylinder（shown as Figure 2-7）.

Basic System Operation

Air enters the engine through the air induction system where it is measured by the air flow meter. As the air flows into the cylinder, fuel is mixed into the air by the fuel injector. Fuel injectors are arranged in the intake manifold behind each intake valve. The ECU signals the injector to deliver just enough fuel to achieve an ideal air/fuel ratio of 14.7∶1. The ECU determines the basic injection quantity based upon measured intake air volume and engine rpm. Depending on engine operating conditions, injection quantity will vary. The ECU monitors variables such as coolant temperature, engine speed, throttle angle, and exhaust oxygen content.

driveability [draivə'bılıtı]
　　　　　　　　　　n.动力性、驱动性
puddle ['pʌdəl]　　　vt.搅浊，胶土

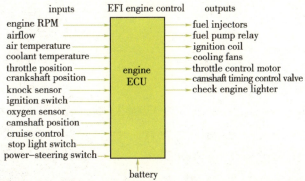

Figure 2-7　Inputs and outputs to and from the ECU for an EFI system

Advantages of EFI (Multipoint Fuel Injection)

Each cylinder has its own injector that delivers fuel directly to the intake valve. This eliminates the need for fuel to travel through the intake manifold, improving cylinder to cylinder distribution. EFI supplies an accurate air/fuel ratio to the engine no matter what operating conditions are encountered.[7] This provides better driveability, fuel economy, and emissions control. By delivering fuel directly at the back of the intake valve, the intake manifold design can be optimized to improve air velocity at the intake valve. This improves torque and throttle response. Cold engine and wide-open throttle enrichment can be reduced with an EFI engine because fuel puddling in the intake manifold is not a problem. This results in better overall fuel economy and improved emissions control. The combination of better fuel atomization and injection directly at the intake valve improves ability to start and run a cold engine.[8] The EFI system does not rely on any major adjustments for cold enrichment or fuel metering. Because the system is mechanically simple, maintenance requirements are reduced.

Proper Names

1. fuel system	燃油供给系
2. fuel tank	燃油箱
3. fuel filter	燃油滤清器
4. fuel line	油管
5. EFI（electronic fuel injection）	电子控制燃油喷射
6. fuel supply system	燃油供给装置
7. air induction system	空气进气系统
8. pressure regulator	压力调节器
9. fuel return pipe	燃油回油管
10. ECU（electronic control unit）	电子控制装置（单元）
11. fuel supply pipe	输油管
12. cold start injector	冷起动喷油器
13. single point fuel injection	单点燃油喷射
14. multipoint fuel injection	多点燃油喷射
15. throttle body injection	节气门体燃油喷射
16. air mass	气团
17. air flow meter	空气流量计
18. plenum chamber	充气室，增压室
19. charcoal canister	活性炭罐
20. outlet valve	出油阀，放出阀
21. engine compartment	发动机舱
22. consists of	由…组成
23. emission control	排放控制

 Notes

[1] Carburetor fuel systems and EFI systems are designed to deliver the fuel mixture to the engine in a combustible form, but each system does it in a different way.

翻译：化油器和电子燃油喷射系统都是用于给发动机输送可燃混合物，但是两个系统工作方式不同。

[2] The fuel supply system consists of the fuel tank, fuel pump, fuel filter, fuel supply pipe, fuel injector, fuel pressure regulator, and fuel return pipe.

翻译：（电喷）燃油供给装置由油箱、燃油泵、燃油滤清器、供油管、喷油器、燃油压力调节器及回油管等组成。

语法：consist of sth.由某事物组成或构成。

例如：the committee consists of ten members. 委员会由十人组成。

区别：consist in sth. 以某事物为其主要的或唯一的因素或特点。

例如：The beauty of the plan consists in its simplicity. 这个计划的好处就在于简单易行。

[3] There are three pipes（or lines）between the fuel tank at the rear of the vehicle and the components in the engine compartment.

翻译：有三根油管，连通汽车后部的油箱和发动机舱内的部件。

[4] A fine gauze filter is fitted to the suction pipe in the fuel tank, and a line filter is fitted in the supply line between the fuel tank and the fuel pump, or between the fuel pump and the carburetor.

翻译：油箱内的吸油管一端装有细滤网油滤器，在油箱和油泵之间的输油管内装有管内滤清器，或者在燃油泵和化油器之间的输油管内安装滤清器。

[5] The air induction system consists of the air cleaner, air flow meter, throttle valve, air intake chamber, intake manifold runner, and intake valve.

翻译：空气进气系统由空气滤清器、空气流量计、节气门、空气进气室、进气歧管总管以及进气门组成。

[6] In the EFI system, it is possible to have systems using only one injector per

engine (single point fuel injection) or one injector per cylinder (multipoint fuel injection).

翻译：在电子燃油喷射系统中，一台发动机可以只使用一个喷油器（单点燃油喷射系统），也可在每个汽缸内使用一个喷油器（多点燃油喷射系统）。

语法：using only one injector...现在分词作后置定语，用来修饰宾语system。

[7] EFI supplies an accurate air/fuel ratio to the engine no matter what operating conditions are encountered.

翻译：在发动机的所有工况下，EFI（电子控制燃油喷射系统）均能提供一个精确的空燃比。

语法：no matter+疑问词引导的从句表示一种让步的从属结构，意为"不论"。

例如：If you don't improve your method, you won't go far, no matter how hard you try. 不论你多么努力尝试，如果不改进方法，是搞不出名堂来的。

[8] The combination of better fuel atomization and injection directly at the intake valve improves ability to start and run a cold engine.

翻译：进气门燃油直接喷射和燃油雾化改善的结合，提高了发动机的冷起动性能和冷机运行性能。

Exercises

1.Choose the best answer from the following choices according to the text.

1) The _____ has the job of supplying a combustible mixture of air and fuel to the engine.

  A. starting system   B. cooling system

  C. lubricating system   D. fuel system

2) Electronic Fuel injection system can be divided into _____ basic sub-systems.

  A. two   B. three   C. four   D. five

3) The length of time that the _____ are open determines the amount of fuel that is sprayed into the engine.

  A. sensors   B. filters   C. injectors   D. pipes

4) The _____ receives signals from the various sensors, processes them and adjusts the amount of fuel that is delivered from the injectors.

A. sensor   B. ECU   C. terminal   D. motor

2. Translate the following words or phrases into Chinese.

1）electronic fuel injection   2）charcoal canister
3）single point fuel injection   4）fuel filter
5）engine startability   6）engine compartment
7）pressure regulator   8）fuel return pipe
9）air flow meter

3. Translate the following words or phrases into English.

1）燃油供给系   2）燃油滤清器
3）空气流量计   4）电子燃油喷射
5）多点燃油喷射   6）冷起动喷油器
7）节气门体燃油喷射   8）空气进气系统
9）输油管

4. Translate the following sentences into Chinese.

1）The fuel system has the job of supplying a combustible mixture of air and fuel to the engine.

2）The purpose of the air induction system is to filter, meter, and measure intake air flow into the engine.

3）Each cylinder has its own injector that delivers fuel directly to the intake valve.

5. Translate the words or phrases in the following figure into Chinese.

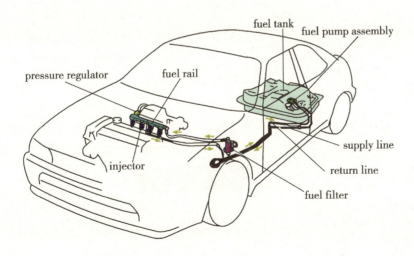

Practical Reading   Engine Measurement and Performance Characteristics

explore [ɪk'splɔ:]　　　v.探测，探究
displacement [dɪs'pleɪsmənt]
　　　　　　　　　n.工作容积，排量
detonation [detə'neɪʃən]　n.爆燃，爆震

The former chapter presented the scientific principles upon which the automobile engine operates. It is time to expand on the topic of engine operation by exploring the many factors that influence engine performance. These factors include bore, stroke, displacement, compression ratio, compression pressure, volumetric efficiency, thermo efficiency, and mechanical efficiency. There are a few negative factors that adversely affect the normal combustion process and can cause power loss and serious engine damage.[1] These factors are, of course, detonation and surface ignition.

Bore

The bore of an engine is a measurement taken inside the cylinder. Actually the bore is the diameter of the cylinder itself. The larger the cylinder bore, of course, the more powerful will be the power stroke because a bigger piston has more area on which the high-pressure combustion gases can push down.

Stroke

Stroke is also a basic cylinder measurement. However, in this case, the measurement is that of the actual piston travel within the cylinder as it moves from TDC to BDC or back again.

A square engine is one that has a bore and stroke of the same dimension; whereas, an oversquare engine has a bore greater than its stroke.[2]

Displacement

Manufacturers commonly use displacement to indicate engine size; this specification is really a measurement of cylinder volume. In other words, when the piston moves up from BDC to TDC, it displaces or pushes away a given volume of gases. Of course, the number of cylinders that an engine has, will determine total engine displacement. Therefore, engine displacement is always equal to the piston displacement of one cylinder multiplied by the number of cylinders in the engine.[3]

Compression Ratio

Another design feature of an engine that determines the total power output of an engine is compression ratio. Compression ratio is a measure of the cylinder volume in cubic inches above the piston when it is at TDC（its clearance volume）compared to the cylinder volume above the piston when it is at BDC. When considering this statement, total cylinder volume appears to be the same thing as piston displacement, but it is not. Total cylinder volume is equal to piston displacement plus combustion chamber volume. The combustion chamber volume, with the piston at top dead center（TDC）is commonly known as clearance volume. Compression ratio is nothing more than the total volume of a cylinder divided by the clearance volume. The formula for finding compression ratio is then（total volume）/（clearance volume）.

Proper Names

1. volumetric efficiency   容积效率
2. thermo efficiency   热效率
3. mechanical efficiency   机械效率
4. surface ignition   表面点火
5. square engine   等径发动机
6. oversquare engine   短行程发动机

Notes

[1] There are a few negative factors that adversely affect the normal combustion process and can cause power loss and serious engine damage.

翻译：一些负面因素会影响发动机的正常燃烧过程，并且导致功率损失和严重的发动机损坏。

[2] A square engine is one that has a bore and stroke of the same dimension; whereas, an oversquare engine has a bore greater than its stroke.

翻译：等径发动机是指发动机的缸径等于活塞行程，短行程发动机的缸径要大于活塞行程。

[3] Therefore, engine displacement is always equal to the piston displacement of one cylinder multiplied by the number of cylinders in the engine.

翻译：因此，发动机排量总是等于单个发动机的排量乘以发动机的汽缸数。

相关链接及网址：
[1] http://www.ford.com/
[2] http://www.a-car.com

推荐书目

[1] 王怡民.汽车专业英语[M].北京：人民交通出版社，2003.
[2] 马林才.汽车实用英语（下）[M].北京：人民交通出版社，2005.

项目3　发动机冷却系和润滑系认识

学习目标

1. 认识关于发动机冷却系和润滑系组成、作用等的英语术语和词汇；
2. 理解发动机冷却系和润滑系的固定表达方法；
3. 运用所学知识，借助词典，对关于冷却系和润滑系等资料进行中英互译；
4. 在教师指导下，完成与发动机冷却系和润滑系相关的英语资料阅读和翻译工作；
5. 正确完成课后练习。

学习时间

4学时

任务描述

以汽油发动机为例，学习有关发动机冷却系的水套、节温器、水泵、散热器、风扇等，以及润滑系中主要零部件等，完成相关术语、词汇、特殊语句的认识。通过完成该任务，能阅读关于发动机冷却和润滑系的英文文献，并能运用所学项目知识，对相关文献进行翻译。

引导问题

你知道下图中的英文代表什么意思吗？

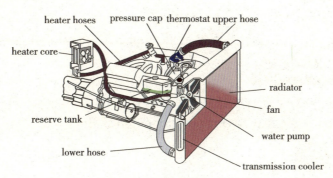

> 学习引导
>
> 本项目的学习，应沿着以下脉络进行：
> 通读全文→学习单词和语法→完成课后练习→分组讨论→课后阅读

Project 3 Acquaintance with Engine Cooling and Lubricating System

Engine Cooling System

A cooling system of some kind is necessary in any internal combustion engine. The cooling system of a water-cooled engine consists of the engine water jacket, thermostat, water pump, radiator, radiator cap, fan, fan drive belt and necessary hoses（shown as Figure 3-1）.

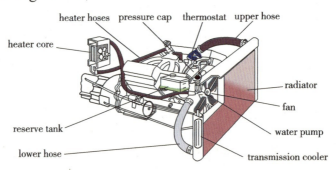

Figure 3-1 Engine cooling system

Heat Transfer

In an automobile engine, heat flows or transfers from the iron or aluminum cylinder to the cooling water, and from the coolant to the copper or aluminum radiator.[1]

Cooling System Pump

Automobile engine water pumps are of many designs, but most are the centrifugal type. Sometimes the fan is installed on the water pump shaft.

Radiator

The radiator is a device designed to dissipate the heat that the coolant has absorbed from the engine. It is constructed to hold a large amount of water in tubes or other passages which provide a large area in contact with the atmosphere （shown as Figure 3-2）.[2]

thermostat ['θəməstæt]
　　　　　　　　n. 节温器，温度自动调节器
transfer [træns'fə:(r)]　　vt. 转移，传递
copper ['kɒpə(r)]　　　　n. 铜，铜制品
centrifugal [sentri'fju:gl]
　　　　　　　　adj. 离心的，离心力的
dissipate ['dɪsɪpeɪt]　　　v. 驱散，消散
idle ['aɪd(ə)l] adj. 空闲的，懒惰的，怠速的
objective [əb'dʒektɪv]　　n. 目标，目的

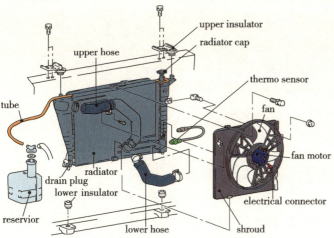

Figure 3-2　Engine radiator assembly components

Radiator Cap

The radiator cap is designed to seal the cooling system so that it operates under some pressure. This improves cooling efficiency and prevents evaporation of the coolant.

Cooling Fan

The fan is designed to draw cooling air through the radiator core. This is necessary at low speeds or when the engine is idling, since there is not enough air motion under those conditions to provide adequate cooling.

Thermostat

Automotive internal combustion engines operate more efficiently when a high temperature is maintained within narrow limits. To attain this objective, a thermostat is inserted in the cooling system. In operation, the thermostat is designed to close off the flow of water from engine to radiator until the engine has reached the desired operating temperature.[3]

Antifreeze Solution

When water freezes, it expands approximately nine percent in volume. Because of this great rate expansion, it will break or serious distort the shape of the vessel in which it is contained. Because of this characteristic, it is necessary to use a nonfreezing solution in the cooling system of water-cooled engines operated in climates where the temperature is below the freezing point of water.[4]

Air-cooled Engine

Air-cooled engines were used successfully in the early days of the automobile. The air should be directed where wanted and the volume of air must be controlled. Forced air circulation is provided by a fan of generous capacity which is usually driven from the engine crankshaft by a belt or by fan blades formed in the flywheel.

Engine Lubricating System

Excessive friction in the engine, however, would mean rapid destruction. We cannot eliminate internal friction, but we can reduce it to a controllable degree by the use of friction reducing lubricants.[5] Lubricating oil in an automobile engine has several tasks to perform:

（1）By lubrication, reduce friction between moving parts of engine.

（2）By acting as a seal to prevent leakage between parts such as pistons, rings and cylinders.

（3）By flowing between friction-generating parts to carry away heat.

（4）By washing away abrasive metal worn from friction surfaces.

Oil is supplied to moving parts of the engine by

Word List

antifreeze ['æntɪfriːz] n. 防冻剂
vessel ['ves(ə)l] n.容器，器皿
climate ['klaɪmɪt] n. 气候，风土
generous ['dʒenərəs] adj. 慷慨的，大方的，大量的
friction ['frɪkʃ(ə)n] n. 摩擦，摩擦力
destruction [dɪ'strʌkʃ(ə)n] n. 破坏，毁灭
lubricant ['luːbrɪkənt] n. 滑润剂
task [tɑːsk] n. 任务，作业
abrasive [ə'breɪsɪv] adj. 研磨的；n. 研磨剂
accumulation [əkjuːmjʊ'leɪʃ(ə)n] n. 积聚，堆积物
detergency [dɪ'təːdʒənsɪ] adj.清净性

pump pressure or splashing, or by a combination of both and reaches the various parts through pipes, passages, drillings, holes and grooves. The oil pump, oil filter and together with oil pan, make up the lubricating system of the engine（shown as Figure 3-3）.

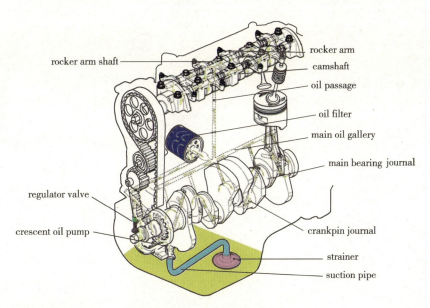

Figure 3-3　Engine lubricating system

Oil Pump

The pumps used to circulate the oil are of the positive displacement type in several designs. Since these pumps handle oil, they are well lubricated at all times and do not suffer from excessive wear. Most cases of lost oil pressure are due to excessive clearance in the bearings of the engine rather than worn oil pumps.[6] Another reason for lack of oil pressure is stoppage in the oil pump supply line or screen. A typical cause is the accumulation of sludge in a screen.

Oil Sludge

Sludge is a mixture of water, oil, dirt and other products of combustion. It is most likely to form in an engine that seldom reaches a satisfactory operating temperature. Slow speed, stop-and-go operation means that the engine seldom gets hot enough to drive the water and vapor out of the crankcase.[7] Sludge formation can be held to a minimum by using the correct cooling system thermostat to maintain a high engine operating temperature. Using engines oils of high detergency and making frequent changes of oil and filter are necessary. Adequate crankcase ventilation is also important（shown as Figure 3-4）.

Word List

varnish ['vɑːnɪʃ]	n. 漆膜，清漆
lacquer ['lækə(r)]	n. 漆膜，涂膜
substance ['sʌbstəns]	n. 物质，实质
regularly ['regjulələr]	adv. 有规律地，有规则地
diluent [dai'ljuːənt]	n. 稀释液，冲淡剂
acid ['æsɪd]	n. 酸
viscosity [vɪs'kɔsɪtɪ]	n. 黏度
corrosion [kə'rəʊʒ(ə)n]	n. 腐蚀
slippery ['slɪpərɪ]	adj. 滑的，光滑的

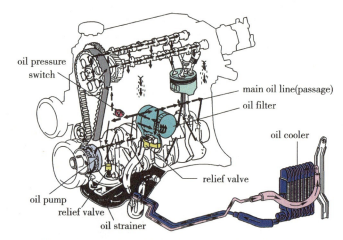

Figure 3-4 Engine lubricating system with oil cooler

Engine Varnish

Another type of engine deposit is known as "varnish" or "lacquer." Varnish or lacquer is formed when an engine is worked hard enough to run hot for extended periods of time.[8] The heat causes the oil to break down, and some of the elements to separate out and deposit as a varnish-like substance on the metal parts. To avoid such deposits, it is necessary to use the best oil obtainable and change oil regularly. It is also essential to make sure that the cooling system is functioning efficiently.

Oil Filter

Oil filter is placed in the engine oil system to remove dirt and abrasives from the oil （shown as Figure 3-5）. Diluents, such as gasoline and acids, are not removed. However, by removing the solid materials, the possibility of acids forming is reduced, and the rate of wear of engine parts is greatly reduced. Oil filters installed on modern passenger car engines are full-flow type; all oil passes through the filter before it reaches the bearings. However, in the event the filter becomes clogged or obstructed, a bypass valve is provided so that oil will continue to reach the bearings.

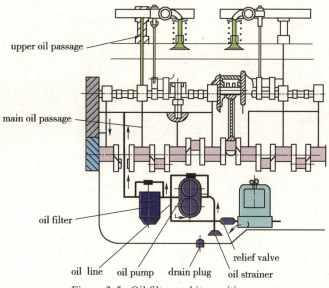

Figure 3-5　Oil filter and its position

🔍 Additives

The requirements of today's automobile engines are far beyond the range of straight mineral oils. Oils used in automobiles need some additives to improve their characteristics. There are many different additives in use today. Pour point depressant is designed to overcome the difficulty of pouring oil in cold weather. Detergent-dispersant additives are used to prevent sludge and varnish deposits. Foam inhibitors are designed to prevent the formation of foam. Oxidation inhibitors are used to reduce the possibility of oil being oxidized. Viscosity index improvers improve the viscosity index. Corrosion and rust inhibitors are designed to help the detergent-dispersant additives in the prevention of rust and corrosion.[9] Antiwear additives have the ability to coat metal surfaces with a strong and slippery film that prevents direct metal-to-metal contact.

🔍 Proper Names

1. cooling system　　　　　　　冷却系
2. lubricating system　　　　　　润滑系
3. radiator cap　　　　　　　　　散热器盖
4. radiator core　　　　　　　　　散热器芯
5. fan blade　　　　　　　　　　　风扇叶片

6. positive displacement type　　　　　容积式
7. oil sludge　　　　　　　　　　　　油泥
8. crankcase ventilation　　　　　　　曲轴箱通风
9. break down　　　　　　　　　　　分解
10. pour point depressant　　　　　　　降凝剂
11. detergent-dispersant　　　　　　　清净分散剂
12. foam inhibitor　　　　　　　　　　抗泡剂
13. oxidation inhibitor　　　　　　　　抗氧剂
14. viscosity index improver　　　　　黏度指数改进剂
15. antiwear additive　　　　　　　　抗磨添加剂
16. in contact with　　　　　　　　　与…在接触中，接触
17. because of　　　　　　　　　　　因为，由于
18. coat with　　　　　　　　　　　　给某物涂、盖、包上
19. suction pipe　　　　　　　　　　　吸油管
20. crescent oil pump　　　　　　　　月牙形齿轮泵
21. regulator valve　　　　　　　　　调压阀

 Notes

[1] In an automobile engine, heat flows or transfers from the iron or aluminum cylinder to the cooling water, and from the coolant to the copper or aluminum radiator.

翻译：在汽车发动机里面，热量从铁或铝制的汽缸传导到冷却水中，再由冷却水将热量传递到铜或铝制的散热器中。

[2] It is constructed to hold a large amount of water in tubes or other passages which provide a large area in contact with the atmosphere.

翻译：在结构上，散热器的管道要能容纳大量水，这些管道能提供较大的与空气接触的散热面积。

语法：which引导定语从句，修饰tubes or passages。

[3] In operation, the thermostat is designed to close off the flow of water from engine to radiator until the engine has reached the desired operating temperature.

翻译：工作时，在发动机还未达到合适的工作温度前，节温器将切断从发动机水套流向散热器的水路。

语法：until the engine has reached the desired operating temperature引导时间

状语从句。

在用法上：A till（until）B 。A所表示的动作或状态一直持续下去，到till（until）B出现时即停止并向相反方向转化。

[4] Because of this characteristic, it is necessary to use a nonfreezing solution in the cooling system of water-cooled engines operated in climates where the temperature is below the freezing point of water.

翻译：由于冷却水在低温时会冻结，所以，水冷式发动机在气温低于水的凝固点以下运行时，需要向冷却系统中加入防冻液。

语法：because of后接短语表原因。

it is necessary to use是it作形式主语，为了避免全句的头重脚轻。真正主语是to不定式，本句亦是To use…is necessary。

[5] We cannot eliminate internal friction, but we can reduce it to a controllable degree by the use of friction reducing lubricants.

翻译：虽然发动机的内摩擦无法消除，但可以通过使用减摩润滑剂，将摩擦减小到一定的程度。

[6] Most cases of lost oil pressure are due to excessive clearance in the bearings of the engine rather than worn oil pumps.

翻译：机油压力不足的大部分情形都是由于发动机内轴承间隙过大造成的，而不主要是由机油泵磨损造成的。

[7] Slow speed, stop-and-go operation means that the engine seldom gets hot enough to drive the water and vapor out of the crankcase.

翻译：低速、停停开开等工况意味着发动机温度较低，无法将曲轴箱内的水汽和蒸汽排出。

语法：that引导的从句作谓语mean的宾语。

[8] Varnish or lacquer is formed when an engine is worked hard enough to run hot for extended periods of time.

翻译：当发动机长时间满负荷运行，导致过热，从而在发动机内形成漆膜状沉积物。

语法：when引导了时间状语从句。

[9] Corrosion and rust inhibitors are designed to help the detergent-dispersant additives in the prevention of rust and corrosion.

翻译：防腐防锈剂有助于清净分散剂防锈蚀和防腐蚀。

Exercises

1. Choose the best answer from the following choices according to the text.

　　1）In an automobile engine, heat flows or transfers from the iron or aluminum cylinder to the cooling water, and from the coolant to the copper or aluminum_____.

　　　　A. pump　　　　B. radiator　　C. piston　　D. fan

　　2）When water freezes, it expands approximately_____percent in volume.

　　　　A. seven　　　　B. eight　　　C. nine　　　D. ten

　　3）Oils used in automobiles need some_____to improve their characteristics.

　　　　A. additives　　　B. antifreeze　　C. lubricant　　D. coolant

2. Translate the following word or phrases into Chinese.

　　1）cooling system　　　2）thermostat　　　3）radiator cap

　　4）radiator core　　　　5）lubricating system　　6）crankcase ventilation

　　7）viscosity index improver　　8）varnish　　　9）oil sludge

3. Translate the following word or phrases into English.

　　1）水泵　　　　　　　2）防冻液　　　　　　3）水冷式发动机

　　4）润滑系　　　　　　5）滑润剂　　　　　　6）抗氧剂

　　7）发动机沉积物　　　8）机油滤清器　　　　9）金属与金属接触

4. Translate the following sentences into Chinese.

　　1）Excessive friction in the engine, however, would mean rapid destruction.

　　2）In order to reduce the formation of rust, commercial antifreeze contains an inhibitor designed to prevent corrosion.

5. Translate the words or phrases in the following figure into Chinese.

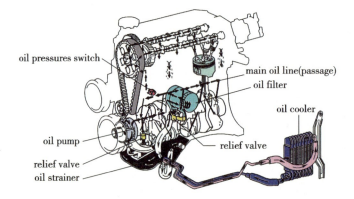

Practical Reading   Cooling-system Problems

Engine overheating, loss of coolant and slow warm-up are the most common problems with cooling systems.

Overheating

Overheating is noticed by a high temperature-gauge reading. The main causes are loss of coolant and accumulation of rust and scale in the system. Coolant that is discoloured or rusty indicates lack of maintenance.

Rust, scale and corrosion that form in the coolant passages will restrict coolant flow and particles carried into the radiator tank will clog the tubes.

Overheating can sometimes be caused by a fault in the ignition or fuel systems. Any loss of power due to a retarded spark or a poor fuel mixture could cause a problem, but poor engine performance should be more noticeable than overheating.[1]

Coolant Loss

Coolant loss is evident by the need to constantly top up the coolant in the reservoir. Bad coolant leaks are easy to find, but leaks which occur only under operating pressure are more difficult to locate and the system would have to be pressure-tested.

External leaks could come from the radiator, water pump, hose connections, or core plugs in the cylinder

Word List

maintenance['mentənəns]
　　　　　　　　n.维护，保持，维修，保养
rust [rʌst]　　　　　　　n.铁锈；vt.（使）生锈
scale [skeil]　　　　　　　　　　　　n.水垢
corrosion [kə'rəuʒən]　　n.侵蚀，腐蚀状态
silicone['sili,kəun]　　　　　　　　n.硅树脂
cavitation [,kævi'teiʃən]　　　　n.气穴现象
electrolysis [ilek'trɔlisis]　　　　　　n.电解

block or head.

Internal leaks could be due to a faulty cylinder head gasket, a cylinder head with a warped surface, or enlarged water passages in the cylinder head and water pump due to corrosion. Other less well-known causes of metal loss are cavitations or electrolysis.

Slow Warm-up

The likely cause of a slow warm-up is that the thermostat is faulty and not closing, or that it has been removed.

The silicone clutch on a variable-speed fan could be faulty, or an electric fan may not be cutting out when the engine is cold. [2]

Proper Names

1. engine overheating   发动机过热
2. coolant loss   冷却液损失
3. slow warm-up   暖机缓慢
4. external leak   外部泄漏
5. internal leak   内部泄漏

Notes

[1] Any loss of power due to a retarded spark or a poor fuel mixture could cause a problem, but poor engine performance should be more noticeable than overheating.

翻译：任何由于点火延迟或者劣质混合气造成的能量损失都会导致发动机过热，不过发动机性能变差则更明显。

[2] The silicone clutch on a variable-speed fan could be faulty, or an electric fan may not be cutting out when the engine is cold.

翻译：变速风扇上的硅油风扇离合器可能会出错，或者发动机冷态的时候电动风扇没有切断。

学习资料

相关链接及网址：

[1] http://280autoservice.com/EngineCoolingSystemService.aspx
[2] http://www.a-car.com

[3] http://www.autorepairintheknow.com/prevent-a-car-from-overheating/

[4] http://ffden-2.phys.uaf.edu/103_fall2003.web.dir/Chris_Peterson/Coolingsystem.htm

推荐书目

[1] 王怡民.汽车专业英语[M].北京：人民交通出版社，2003.

[2] 马林才.汽车实用英语（下）[M].北京：人民交通出版社，2005.

项目4　汽车底盘构造认识

学习目标

1. 认识汽车底盘中关于传动系、行驶系、转向系和制动系等的英语术语和词汇；
2. 理解汽车底盘各系统中零部件及其工作过程的英语固定表达的方法；
3. 运用所学知识，借助专业词典，对关于汽车底盘构造资料进行中英互译；
4. 在教师指导下，完成与汽车底盘构造及工作过程相关的英语资料阅读和翻译工作；
5. 正确完成课后练习。

学习时间

6学时

任务描述

以民用汽车为例，学习有关变速器、离合器、差速器、传动轴、制动器、轮胎和悬架等汽车底盘知识，完成相关术语、词汇、特殊语句的认识。通过完成该任务，能阅读关于汽车底盘构造及工作过程的英文文献，并能运用所学项目知识和翻译技巧，翻译相关文献。

引导问题

你知道下图中的英文代表什么意思吗？

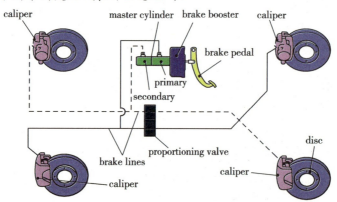

Project 4　Acquaintance with Automotive Chassis Construction

Motor vehicles vary greatly in design and body style, and the term motor vehicle can be used to include passenger cars, station wagons, vans, utilities, trucks, buses and coaches. For passenger cars and light commercial vehicles, there are two basic arrangements: front-wheel drive and rear-wheel drive. A motor vehicle consists of a number of sections which, for convenience, can be considered as follows: the engine assembly, the frame or chassis, the power train, the running gear, the electrical system and the body of the vehicle（shown as Figure 4-1）.

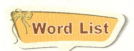

Word List	
chassis ['ʃæsɪ]	n.底盘
passenger ['pæsɪndʒə]	n.乘客，旅客
van [væn]	n.大篷货车，运货车
coach [kəutʃ]	n.长途客车
frame [freɪm]	n.车架
handbrake ['hænd'breɪk]	n.驻车制动器
transmission [trænz'mɪʃən]	n.变速器
clutch [klʌtʃ]	n.离合器
differential [dɪfə'renʃəl]	n.差速齿轮，差速器

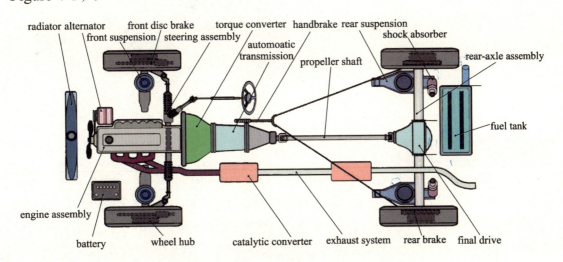

Figure 4-1　Arrangement of a rear-wheel-drive vehicle

The power train carries power from the engine crankshaft to the car wheels so the wheels rotate and car moves.[1] The power train includes transmission, clutch, differential and drive shaft.

Manual Transmission

The manual transmission provides a means of varying the relationship between the speed of the engine and the speed of the wheels. Varying these gear ratios allows the right amount of engine power at many different speeds. Manual transmission requires use of a clutch to apply and remove the engine torque to the transmission input shaft.

A basic transmission has seven gears of various sizes which are carried on three shafts. As well as this, there is a reverse idler gear and shaft which are not included in the illustration. Most manual transmissions have four or five forward speeds and, of course, more gearing and associated parts. The shafts that carry the gears are: the input shaft, the countershaft （or cluster）, the main shaft （or output shaft） and the reverse idler shaft （shown as Figure 4-2）.

Word List

torque [tɔːk]　　　　　　　n.扭矩，转矩
illustration[ˌiləˈstreiʃən]　n.插图，图表，图案
countershaft[ˈkauntəʃɑːft]　n.中间轴
disconnect [ˌdiskəˈnekt]
　　　　　　　　　v.断开，分离，拆开

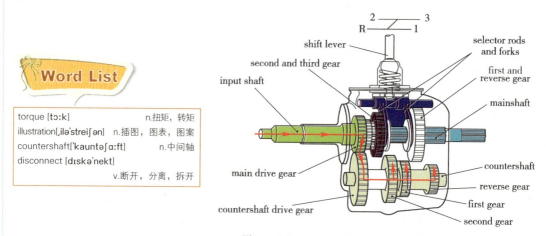

Figure 4-2　A typical manual transmission construction

Clutch

The clutch allows you to connect and disconnect the engine and the transmission, both starting up and during shifts （shown as Figure 4-3）. A single-disc clutch assembly consists of four main parts: the rear face of the flywheel, the clutch disc, the pressure-plate assembly, the release mechanism. As well as this, there are the clutch controls between the clutch pedal and the release mechanism.

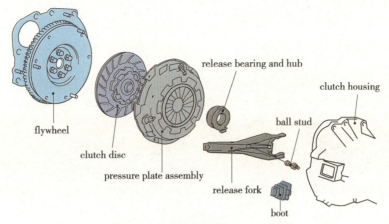

Figure 4-3 The clutch components

🔍 Automatic Transmission

In an automatic transmission, gear ratios are changed automatically. This eliminates the need for the driver to operate the clutch and manually "shift gears". The typical automatic transmission combines a fluid torque converter, a planetary gear system, and a hydraulic control system in a single unit (shown as Figure 4-4).

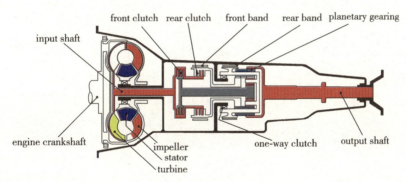

Figure 4-4 Torque converter and mechanical components in an automatic transmission

🔍 Drive Shaft

The drive shaft connects the transmission output shaft to the differential pinion shaft （shown as Figure 4-5）. Since all roads are not perfectly smooth, and the transmission is fixed, the drive shaft has to be flexible to absorb the shocks of bumps in the road.[2] Universal, or "U-joints" allow the drive shaft to flex when the drive angle changes.

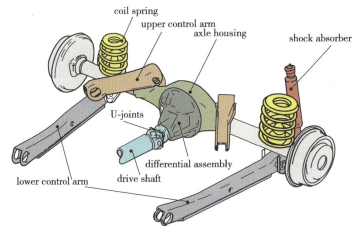

Figure 4-5 Rear axle with drive shaft, differential and coil spring suspension

Final Drive and Differential

A typical differential carrier assembly includes the final-drive gears (the crown wheel and pinion), the differential case and the differential gears. These parts, which are all supported by bearings in the differential carrier, are usually referred to as the differential assembly (shown as Figure 4-6).

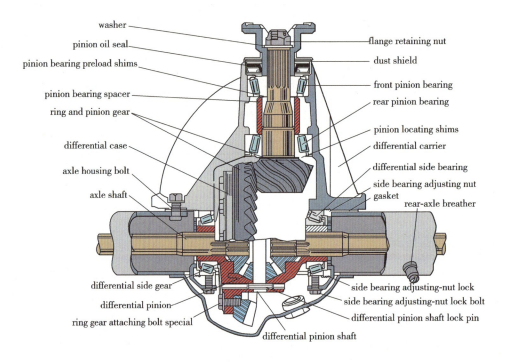

Figure 4-6 Typical final drive and differential assembly

Differential

Differentials are used at the rear of vehicles with rear-wheel drive and used at the front in the transaxles of vehicles with front-wheel drive. When the car is on straight road, the ring gear, differential case, differential pinion gears, and two differential side gears all turn as a unit without any relative motion.[3] However, when the car begins to round a curve, the differential pinion gears rotate on the pinion shaft. This permits the outer wheel to turn faster than the inner wheel.

Word List

shift [ʃɪft]	vt.换挡，替换，改变，变速
impeller [ɪmˈpelə]	n.泵轮
stator [ˈsteɪtə]	n.导轮
turbine [ˈtɜːbɪn]	n.涡轮
axle [ˈæksəl]	n.轴，轮轴，车轴，车桥
suspension [səˈspenʃən]	n.悬架，悬架装置
transaxle [trænsˈæksəl]	n.驱动桥
round [raʊnd]	vt.绕行，拐弯
spoke [spəʊk]	n.轮辐
cab [kæb]	n.驾驶室

Steering System

The steering system must deliver precise directional control. And it must do so requiring little driver effort at the steering wheel. The key components that make up the steering system are the steering wheel, steering column, steering shaft, steering gear, pitman arm, drag link, steering arm, ball joints, and tie-rod assembly（shown as Figure 4-7 and Figure 4-8）.

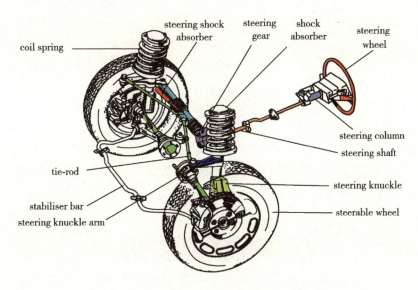

Figure 4-7 Steering system

accommodate [ə'kɔmədeit]	
	vt. 使适应，容纳
angular ['æŋgjulə]	adj. 有角的
gearbox ['giəbɔks]	n. 齿轮箱，变速器
multiply ['mʌltiplai]	v. 乘，增加
worm [wə:m]	n. 蜗杆
roller ['rəulə]	n. 蜗轮，滚筒
socket ['sɔkit]	n. 窝，孔，插座
thread [θred]	n. 螺纹
stud [stʌd]	n. 柱头螺栓，螺柱
unison ['ju:nisən]	n. 和谐，一致

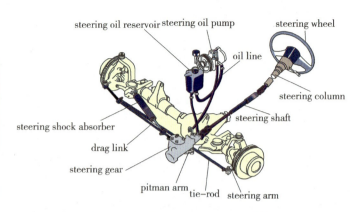

Figure 4-8 Power-steering assembly

Steering Wheel

This is the driver's link to the entire system. The wheel is formed of a strong steel rod shaped into a wheel. Spokes extend from the wheel to the wheel hub, which is fastened securely at the top of the steering column.[4] The wheel assembly is covered with rubber or plastic.

Steering Column

This is a hollow tube that extends from the steering wheel through the floorboard. It is fastened to the cab at or under the instrument panel and contains bearings to support the steering shaft.

Steering Shaft

The steering shaft is basically a rod, usually jointed, that runs from the top of the steering column to the steering gear. U-joints in the shaft accommodate any angular variations between the steering shaft and the steering gear input shaft.

Steering Gear

This gearbox multiplies steering torque and changes its direction as received through the steering shaft from the steering wheel. There are two widely used types of gears: worm and roller, and recirculating ball.

Pitman Arm

The pitman arm is a steel arm clamped to the output shaft of the steering gear. The outer end of the pitman arm moves through an arc in order to change the rotary motion of the steering gear output shaft into linear motion.[5] The length of the pitman arm affects steering quickness. A longer pitman arm will generate more steering motion at the front wheels for a given amount of steering wheel movement.

Drag Link

This forged rod connects the pitman arm to the steering arm. The drag link is connected at each end by ball joints.

Steering Arm

Sometimes called a steering lever, this forged steel component connects the drag link to the top portion of the driver's side steering knuckle and spindle.[6] As the steering arm moves, it changes the angle of the steering knuckle.

Ball Joints

This ball-and-socket assembly consists of a forged steel ball with a threaded stud attached to it. A socket shell grips the ball. The ball stud moves around to provide the freedom of movement needed for various steering links to accommodate relative motion between the axle and the frame rail when the front axle springs flex.

Tie-Rod Assembly

The steering arm or lever controls the movement of the driver's side steering knuckle. There must be some method of transferring this steering motion to the opposite, passenger side steering knuckle. This is done through the use of a tie-rod assembly that links the two steering knuckles together and forces them to act in unison.

Brake System

A braking system consists of two main sections. These are the brake assemblies at the wheels and the hydraulic system that applies the brakes. The system includes the service（foot）brakes for use when the vehicle is being driven, and a parking brake, usually hand operated, which is applied when the vehicle is parked (shown as Figure 4-9). The automobile brake systems are divided into three types of service brake combinations: drum brakes, disc brakes, and disc-drum combinations. Some systems have disc brakes at all four wheels, some have disc brakes at the front and drum brakes at the rear, others have drum brakes at all four wheels.

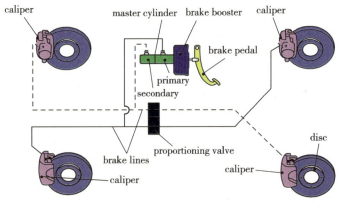

Figure 4-9　Arrangement of a basic brake system

Drum Brake

Drum brakes use an internal expanding brake shoe with the lining attached, working within the confines of a rotating brake surface called a brake drum.[7] The brake shoe diameter is expanded to contact the brake surface by a hydraulic cylinder that is referred to as a wheel cylinder. Fluid pressure from the master cylinder supplies fluid to the wheel cylinders causing them to expand. The expansion of the wheel cylinder through mechanical linkage forces the brake linings into contact with the rotating brake drum to provide braking action (shown as Figure 4-10).

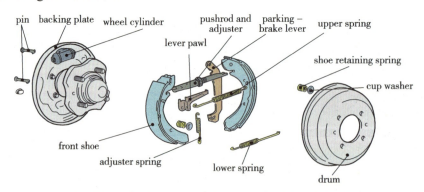

Figure 4-10　Dismantled rear drum-brake assembly with parking-brake parts

Disc Brake

Disc brakes employ a brake disc that rotates with the wheel. The brake disc is usually referred to as a brake rotor (shown as Figure 4-11). A hydraulically operated caliper is used to force the lining friction material against the braking surface of the rotor for stopping wheel rotation.[8]

diameter [daiˈæmɪtə]	n. 直径
caliper [ˈkælɪpə]	n. 卡钳
wishbone [ˈwiʃbəun]	n. 叉形臂

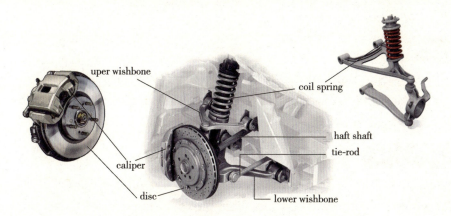

Figure 4-11　Disc brake and related suspension components

Hydraulic Brake System

Hydraulic brake systems utilize liquid to transfer force from the driver's foot to the brake shoes. Depressing the brake pedal creates a mechanical force that is transmitted through a pushrod to a piston in the master cylinder. The piston, in turn, pushes the brake fluid through the brake lines to pistons in a caliper or a cylinder on each wheel. The pressure acting on these pistons pushes brake shoes against a rotating disc or drum. This friction generated by the contacting brake shoes and rotating disc/drum, slows and eventually stops the wheels. Releasing the brake pedal causes this action to reverse-with brake fluid returning to the master cylinder (shown as Figure 4-12).

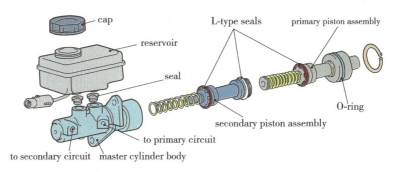

Figure 4-12　Dismantled master cylinder of hydraulic brake system

Air Brake System

The second type of system, the air brake system, utilizes compressed air as a source of force to stop the truck. A complete air brake system includes foundation brakes, air system and optional brake equipment.

Parking Brakes

The parking brake system is used to hold one or more of the vehicle brakes in an applied position for an extended period of time. This brake system must be capable of holding the vehicle on a grade and bringing the vehicle to a stop if the service brakes fail.[9]

Tires and Wheels

Tires and wheels are important to vehicle ride, handling, and fuel economy. The tires and wheels must firstly support the vehicle weight. The tires are also required to change the vehicle direction while the vehicle is in motion. In addition, the tires and wheels have to transfer the engine and braking torque to the road surface for driving and braking the vehicle. As far as construction is concerned, there are two basic types of tires: bias or cross-ply and radial (shown as Figure 4-13). The difference is the way in which the cords in the plies are arranged.

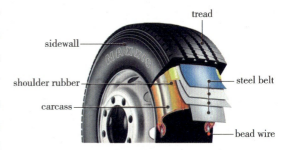

Figure 4-13　Tire construction

Suspension System

The suspension components include the springs, axle, shock absorbers, arms, rods and ball joints. These suspend the body and associated parts so that they are insulated from road shocks and vibrations which would otherwise be transferred to the passengers and load. Parts of front suspensions also perform steering functions. The springs used on today's cars and trucks include leaf springs, coil springs, air springs, and torsion bars（shown as Figure 4-14）.

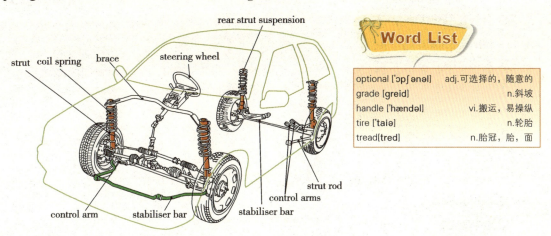

Figure 4-14 Passenger cars with independent suspension on all four wheels

Proper Names

1. power train 　　　　　　　　传动系统
2. drive shaft 　　　　　　　　传动轴
3. manual transmission 　　　　手动变速器
4. automatic transmission 　　　自动变速器
5. planetary gear system 　　　行星齿轮系统
6. differential case 　　　　　　差速器壳
7. differential pinion gears 　　差速器行星小齿轮
8. differential side gears 　　　差速器半轴齿轮
9. propeller shaft 　　　　　　传动轴
10. universal joint 　　　　　　万向节
11. steering system 　　　　　　转向系
12. brake system 　　　　　　　制动系
13. steering wheel 　　　　　　转向盘
14. steering column 　　　　　转向管柱
15. steering shaft 　　　　　　转向轴
16. steering gear 　　　　　　　转向器，转向齿轮
17. pitman arm 　　　　　　　转向摇臂

18. drag link   转向直拉杆
19. steering arm   转向节臂
20. ball joint   球形接头
21. tie-rod   转向横拉杆
22. steering knuckle   转向节
23. service brake system   行车制动系
24. parking brake system   驻车制动系
25. drum brake   鼓式制动器
26. disc brake   盘式制动器
27. brake shoe   制动蹄
28. wheel cylinder   轮缸，分泵
29. master cylinder   主缸，总泵
30. hydraulic brake system   液压制动系统
31. brake pedal   制动踏板
32. suspension system   悬架系统
33. leaf spring   钢板弹簧
34. coil spring   螺旋弹簧
35. air spring   空气弹簧，减振气囊
36. torsion bar   扭杆弹簧
37. make up   弥补，整理，化妆，拼凑
38. passenger car   乘用车
39. station wagon   旅行车
40. running gear   行驶系
41. Commercial vehicles   商用车
42. reverse idler gear   倒挡中间齿轮
43. release mechanism   分离机构
44. clutch control   离合器控制装置
45. cross-ply tire   斜交轮胎
46. shock absorber   减振器
47. torque converter   液力变矩器
48. wheel hub   轮毂
49. catalytic converter   催化转换器
50. final drive   主减速器
51. shift lever   换挡杆
52. selector rods and fork   选挡杆与拨叉

53.clutch housing　　　　　离合器壳
54.release fork　　　　　　分离拨叉
55.one-way clutch　　　　　单向离合器
56.axle housing　　　　　　桥壳
57.stabilizer bar　　　　　横向稳定杆
58.strut rod　　　　　　　 支撑杆
59.radial tire　　　　　　 子午线轮胎
60.cord ply　　　　　　　 帘布层

Notes

[1] The power train carries power from the engine crankshaft to the car wheels so the wheels rotate and car moves.

翻译：从发动机曲轴输出的动力经传动系传递给车轮，使车轮转动，驱动汽车行驶。

[2] Since all roads are not perfectly smooth, and the transmission is fixed, the drive shaft has to be flexible to absorb the shocks of bumps in the road.

翻译：由于路面并非全部都是平整的，同时变速器的位置是固定的，所以，传动轴必须具备一定的柔韧性，以吸收来自路面的颠簸振动。

语法：since…引导原因状语从句。

[3] When the car is on straight road, the ring gear, differential case, differential pinion gears, and two differential side gears all turn as a unit without any relative motion.

翻译：当汽车在直线道路上行驶时，齿圈、差速器壳、差速器行星小齿轮以及差速器半轴齿轮等作为一个无相对运动的整体而转动。

语法：when引导时间状语从句。as a unit表示运动的方式。

[4] Spokes extend from the wheel to the wheel hub, which is fastened securely at the top of the steering column.

翻译：转向盘辐条从转向盘轮缘延伸到转向盘的轮毂，轮毂则被紧固在转向管柱的顶端。

语法：which is fastened securely at the top of the steering column是非限定性定语从句，用于修饰先行词the wheel hub。

[5] The outer end of the pitman arm moves through an arc in order to change the

rotary motion of the steering gear output shaft into linear motion.

翻译：转向摇臂的外端作弧线运动，以便将转向器输出轴的旋转运动转变成直线运动。

[6] Sometimes called a steering lever, this forged steel component connects the drag link to the top portion of the driver's side steering knuckle and spindle.

翻译：钢制的转向节臂又称为转向杆，将转向直拉杆与驾驶员侧的转向节和转向轮轴的上端部分连接在一起。

[7] Drum brakes use an internal expanding brake shoe with the lining attached, working within the confines of a rotating brake surface called a brake drum.

翻译：鼓式制动器使用一个内张型的带摩擦片的制动蹄，制动蹄上的摩擦片与一个称为制动鼓的旋转的制动表面的一定区域相接触（产生制动力）。

语法：working…是现在分词短语，作用相当于状语从句。

[8] A hydraulically operated caliper is used to force the lining friction material against the braking surface of the rotor for stopping wheel rotation.

翻译：液压式制动钳是用来迫使摩擦片上摩擦材料紧靠在制动盘的端面上，以使车轮停止旋转。

[9] This brake system must be capable of holding the vehicle on a grade and bringing the vehicle to a stop if the service brakes fail.

翻译：如果行车制动系统失效，驻车制动系统必须能保证汽车在斜坡上原地停驻。

语法：be capable of doing中的doing即为句中的holding和bringing，它们是并列关系。

Exercises

1.Choose the best answer from the following choices according to the text.

1）In an automatic transmission, _____ are changed automatically.

  A. torque B. directions C. shifts D. gear ratios

2）Manual transmission requires use of a _____ to apply and remove the engine torque to the transmission input shaft.

  A. chassis B. differential C. clutch D. axle

3）The steering gear multiplies steering _____ and changes its direction as received through the steering shaft from the steering wheel.

  A. power B. torque C. friction D. wheel

  4）Hydraulic brake systems utilize _____ to transfer force from the driver's foot to the brake shoes.

  A. air B. liquid C. solid D. linkage

  5）The _____ connects the transmission output shaft to the differential pinion shaft.

  A. shift lever B. stabilizer bar C. drive shaft D. Suspension

2. Translate the following words or phrases into Chinese.

  1）pitman arm 2）automatic transmission 3）planetary gear system

  4）chassis 5）universal joint 6）steering system

  7）brake system 8）service brake system 9）parking brake system

3. Translate the following words or phrases into English.

  1）传动系 2）手动变速器 3）差速器

  4）后轮驱动 5）转向盘 6）钢板弹簧

  7）制动蹄 8）悬架系统 9）制动踏板

4. Translate the following sentences into Chinese.

  1）The universal joint or U-joint is used to connect the drive shaft to the transmission output shaft.

  2）Truck steering systems are either manual or power assisted, with power assist units using either hydraulic or air assist setups to make steering effort easier.

  3）The larger the steering wheel diameter, the more torque is generated from the same amount of drive effort.

5. Translate the words or phrases in the following figure into Chinese.

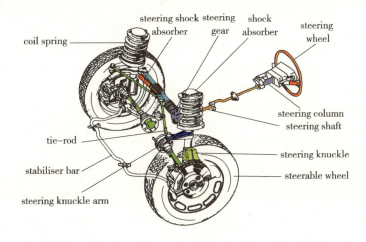

Practical Reading The Introduction of Electronically Controlled Air Suspension

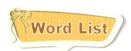

compressor [kəm'presə]　　　n.压缩机
discharge [dis'tʃɑ:dʒ]
　　　　　　vt.释放,排出　vi.排出，放电
voltage ['vəultidʒ]　　　　　n.电压
potentiometer [pə,tenʃi'ɔmitə]
　　　　　　　　　　n.电位计,分压计
irrespective [,iris'pektiv]
　　　　　　a.（of）不考虑的，不顾及的

The electronically controlled air suspension (ECAS) system allows different ride heights to be either manually or automatically selected. By changing the volume of air in each of the air springs, the system maintains ride height and quality regardless of load.[1] System components are as follows:

ASU – Air Supply Unit

The ASU supplies clean dry air and distributes it to the air springs, which includes the following major parts; A compressor for supply of compressed air to the air springs. The compressor assembly includes a solenoid exhaust valve to enable air released from the springs to be discharged to atmosphere.

An electronic control unit is for control of the ECAS system. A dryer / filter to ensure that the air supplied to the springs is clean and dry. Electrical solenoid valves for distribution of air to and from the springs, and to and from an air reservoir（if fitted）.

Height Sensors

Height sensors are mounted between the chassis and the axle. These provide a voltage signal to the ECU that varies as the distance between the chassis and the axle varies, e.g. as happens when the vehicle is being loaded or unloaded.[2] More precisely, the connecting rod and arm translate changes in the distance between the chassis and the axle into rotation of an electrical potentiometer inside the sensor body. As the potentiometer rotates so the output signal from it changes.

 Air Springs

The primary aim of the Air Spring is to have a spring element that ensures a constantly low natural frequency of the vehicle body, irrespective of load, thereby providing excellent ride comfort. The solution comprises the combined action of spring elements and in conjunction with ECAS control automatic level. Together they ensure that vehicle bodies are suspended flexibly and kept at a constant ride heightwhatever the load.

 Proper Names

1. electronically-controlled air suspension　　电子控制空气悬架
2. air supply unit　　空气供给单元
3. solenoid valve　　电磁阀
4. in conjunction with　　与…配合

Notes

[1] By changing the volume of air in each of the air springs, the system maintains ride height and quality regardless of load.
翻译：无论负载多少，通过改变每个空气弹簧的空气量，系统能保持车辆正常行驶的高度和性能。

[2] These provide a voltage signal to the ECU that varies as the distance between the chassis and the axle varies, e.g. as happens when the vehicle is being loaded or unloaded.
翻译：高度传感器给ECU提供的电压信号随着底盘和车轴之间的距离变化而变化，如在车辆正在加载或卸载时发生高度变化。

 学习资料

相关链接及网址：
[1] http://en.wikipedia.org/wiki/Manual_transmission

[2] http://auto.howstuffworks.com/transmission.htm/printable

[3] http://www.csa.com/discoveryguides/auto/review4.php

[4] http://www.gaosun.net/showBrand.jsp

推荐书目

[1] 王怡民.汽车专业英语[M].北京：人民交通出版社，2003.

[2] 马林才.汽车实用英语（下）[M].北京：人民交通出版社，2005.

[3] 赵金祥.汽车底盘构造与维修[M].北京：北京航空航天大学出版社，2008.

[4] 汤姆·伯奇，查克·罗克伍德.汽车手动传动系与驱动桥[M].4版.马林才等，译.北京：中国劳动社会保障出版社，2006.

项目5　汽车电气设备和主动安全系统介绍

学习目标

1. 认识关于汽车电气设备与汽车主动安全系统相关的英语术语和词汇；
2. 理解汽车电气设备与汽车主动安全系统的惯用表达方法；
3. 运用所学知识，借助专业词典，对汽车电气设备以及汽车主动安全系统各大总成进行中英互译；
4. 在教师指导下，完成与汽车主动安全系统相关的英语资料阅读和翻译工作；
5. 正确完成课后练习。

学习时间

6学时

任务描述

介绍汽车上常见的电气设备元件结构及工作原理，如点火系、起动系、发电机、起动机、灯光信号及照明系统等；介绍汽车常见的主动安全系统，如防抱死制动系统，电子稳定程序等。通过完成该任务，能阅读关于汽车电气设备以及汽车主动安全系统的相关英文资料，并掌握相应内容的翻译技巧。

引导问题

你知道下图中的英文代表什么意思吗？

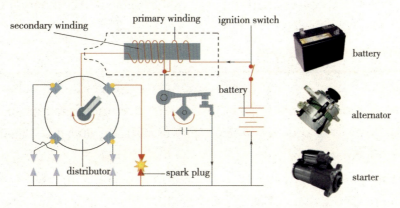

> 学习引导
>
> 本项目的学习，应沿着以下脉络进行：
>
> 通读全文→学习单词和语法→完成课后练习→分组讨论→课后阅读

Project 5 Introduction to the Automotive Electric System and Active Safety Systems

Part I Automotive Electric System

Ignition System

There are many different types of ignition systems. Most of these systems can be placed into one of three distinct groups: the conventional breaker point type ignition systems; the electronic ignition systems; and the distributorless ignition system.

The automotive ignition system has two basic functions: it must control the spark and timing of the spark plug firing to match varying engine requirements, and it must increase battery voltage to a point where it will overcome the resistance offered by the spark plug gap and fire the plug.[1]

The need for higher mileage, reduced emissions and greater reliability has led to the development of the electronic ignition systems. In a distributorless ignition system, the spark plugs are fired directly from the coils. The spark timing is controlled by an Ignition Control Unit（ICU）and the Engine Control Unit（ECU）. The distributorless ignition system may have one coil per cylinder, or one coil for each pair of cylinders.

Ignition System Timing

The goal of the ignition system on your car is to ignite the fuel at exactly the right time so that the expanding gases can do the maximum amount of work. If the ignition system fires at the wrong time, power will fall and gas consumption and emissions can increase.

When the fuel/air mixture in the cylinder burns, the temperature rises and the fuel is converted to exhaust gas. This transformation causes the pressure in the cylinder to increase dramatically and forces the piston down.

In order to get the most torque and power from the engine, the goal is to maximize the pressure in the cylinder during the power stroke. Maximizing pressure will also produce the best engine efficiency, which translates directly into better mileage. The timing of the spark is critical to success.

To make the best use of the fuel, the spark should occur before the piston reaches the top of the compression stroke, so by the time the piston starts down into its power stroke, the pressures are high enough to start producing useful work.[2]

Word List

active ['æctiv]
    adj.积极的,主动的,活动的,
        活跃的,活性的
ignition [ig'niʃən]
   n.点火,点火器,[化]灼热,[机]发火装置
distinct [dis'tiŋct]
    adj.明显的,清晰的,不同的
voltage ['vəultidʒ]　　　　　　n. 电压
resistance [ri'zistəns]　　n. [电] 阻抗, 电阻
emission [i'miʃən]　　　　n. 排放（物）
reliability [ri,laiə'biliti]　　　　n.可靠性
coil [kɔil] n.线圈［盘，架］，线组,感应器
transformation [,trænsfə'meiʃən]
    n.变化,转化,改造,改革,转换
dramatically [drə'mætikəli]
    adv.戏剧地,引人注目地
occur [ə'kə:]　　　　　vi.发生; 举行; 存在
electricity [ilek'trisiti]　　　n.电, 电流
insulated ['isjuleitid]　　adj.绝缘的; 隔热的

Spark Plug

The spark plug is quite simple in theory: It forces electricity to arc across a gap. The electricity must be at a very high voltage in order to travel across the gap and create a good spark. Voltage at the spark plug can be anywhere from 40,000 to 100,000 volts.

The spark plug must have an insulated passageway for this high voltage to travel down to the electrode, where it can jump the gap and, from there, be conducted into the engine block and grounded.[3] The plug also has to withstand the extreme heat and pressure inside the cylinder, and must be designed so that deposits from fuel additives do not build up on the plug.

Ignition System Coil

The coil is a simple device-actually a high-voltage transformer made up of two coils of wire. One coil of wire is called the primary coil. Wrapped around it is the secondary coil. The secondary coil normally has hundreds of times more turns of wire

winding ['waidiŋ]	n. 卷，线圈
solenoid ['səulinɔid]	
n.[电]螺线管,螺线管线圈,电磁线圈；电磁铁	
inhibitor [in'hibitə]	n.抑制物，约束者
electromagnet [ilektrəu'mægnit]	
	n.电磁石，电磁体
plunger ['plʌndʒə]	n.橡胶吸盘，活塞，柱塞
spline [splain]	n.花键;vt.用花键连接,开键槽
armature ['ɑːmətʃə]	n.电枢，转子

than the primary coil.

Current flows from the battery through the primary winding of the coil. The primary coil's current can be suddenly disrupted by the breaker points, or by a solid-state device in an electronic ignition.

Distributorless Ignition

Distributorless ignition does not have a distributor and a single ignition coil. Instead, it uses separate ignition coil packs to provide high secondary voltage directly to the spark plugs. A distributorless ignition system is shown as Figure 5-1. The coil pack includes the separate ignition coils and an ignition driver module. The number of ignition coils is exactly half the number of engine cylinders. This system is also referred to as direct-fire ignition. Each coil provides a spark for two of the cylinders. This is arranged by connecting each end of the secondary winding of the coil to a different spark plug. This causes both plugs to fire at the same time-one spark is used for ignition and the other is wasted.

The pairs of cylinders that receive a spark together are referred to as companion cylinder. One spark plug fires with a forward current flow, but its companion spark plug fires with a reverse current flow.

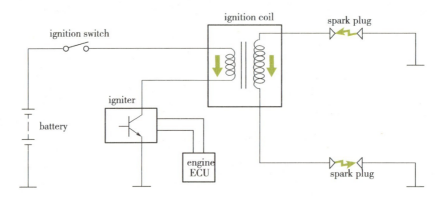

Figure 5-1 The distributorless ignition system

The Starting System

The starting system includes the battery, starter motor, solenoid, ignition switch, and in some cases, a starter relay. A typical starting system is shown as Figure 5-2. An inhibitor （neutral safety） switch is included in the starting system circuit to prevent the vehicle from being started while in gear.

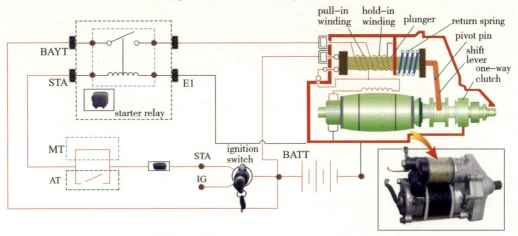

Figure 5-2 A typical starting system

When the ignition key is turned to the start position, current flows and energizes the starter's solenoid coil. The energized coil becomes an electromagnet which pulls the plunger into the coil; the plunger closes a set of contacts which allow high current to reach the starter motor.[4] On models where the solenoid is mounted on the starter, the plunger also serves to push the starter pinion to mesh with the teeth on the flywheel.

In a typical starting system, a battery provides electricity to operate the starter. The ignition switch controls the energizing of the starter relay or solenoid. The starter relay or solenoid makes and breaks the circuit between the battery and starter. The starter converts electrical energy into mechanical energy to rotate the engine. The starter drive gear transmits the starter rotation to the engine flywheel.

To prevent damage to the starter motor when the engine starts, the pinion gear incorporates a one-way clutch which is splined to the starter armature shaft.[5] The rotation of the running engine may speed the rotation of the pinion but not the starter motor itself.

The starting of the engine signals the driver to release the ignition key from the start position, stopping the flow of current to the solenoid or relay. The plunger is pulled out of contact with the battery-to-starter cables by a coil spring, and the flow of electricity is interrupted to the starter.[6]This weakens the magnetic fields and the starter ceases its rotation. As the solenoid plunger is released, its movement also pulls the starter drive gear from its engagement with the engine flywheel. Figure 5-3 shows a cut-away view of a typical starter.

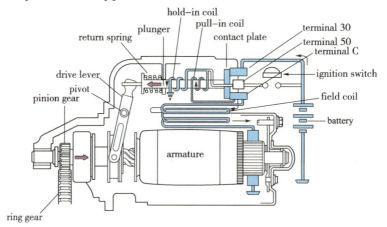

Figure 5-3 Cut-away view of a typical starter system

The Charging System

The charging system provides electrical energy for all the electrical components of the vehicle. The battery provides the electrical energy for starting, but once the engine is running, the alternator supplies all the electrical components of the vehicle. It also charges the battery to replace the energy that is used to start the engine.

The main parts of the charging system include the alternator and its regulator, the drive belt, the battery, a charge warning or indicator light, and the wiring that connects the components of the system. Figure 5-4 shows a cut-away view of a typical alternator.

Word List

alternator ['ɔ:ltə(:)neitə]	n.交流发电机
stabilize ['steibilaiz]	v.使稳定
traction ['trækʃən]	n.牵引力，附着力
stability [stə'biliti]	n.稳定性
intervene [,intə'vi:n]	vi.干涉，干预，介入，调停，插入，阻挠
nerve-wracking ['nə:v,rækiŋ]	adj.极端令人头疼的，非常伤脑筋的
skidding ['skidiŋ]	n.滑行，打滑

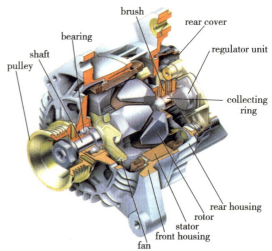

Figure 5-4 Cut-away view of a typical alternator

Part II Automotive Active Safety Systems

The best protection against crashes is to prevent them. Active safety systems help to prevent accidents and thus make a preventative contribution to road safety.[7] They stabilize the vehicle's handling response in critical situations and thus maintain its steer ability. Active safety systems such as the Antilock Braking System ABS, the Traction Control System TCS or the Electronic Stability Program ESP intervene before a crash occurs.

The Antilock Braking System ABS

Stopping a car in a hurry on a slippery road can be very challenging. Anti-lock braking systems (ABS) take a lot of the challenge out of this sometimes nerve-wracking event. In fact, on slippery surfaces, even professional drivers can't stop as quickly without ABS as an average driver can with ABS.[8] A typical Anti-lock system is shown as Figure 5-5.

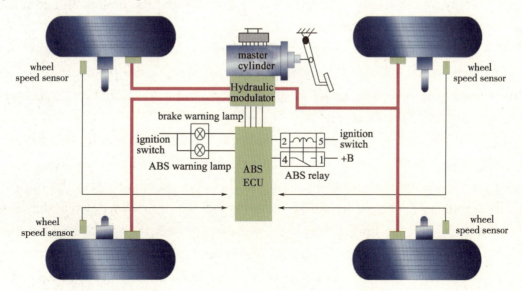

Figure 5-5 Anti-lock brake system

The theory behind anti-lock brakes is simple. A skidding wheel (where the tire contact patch is sliding relative to the road) has less traction than a non-skidding wheel.[9] If you have been stuck on ice, you know that if your wheels are spinning you have no traction. This is because the contact patch is sliding relative to the ice. By keeping the wheels from skidding while you slow down, anti-lock brakes benefit you in two ways: You'll stop faster, and you'll be able to steer while you stop.

There are four main components to an ABS system:

- Wheel speed sensors
- Electronic control unit
- Hydraulic modulator

Wheel Speed Sensors

The anti-lock braking system needs some way of knowing when a wheel is about to lock up. The wheel speed sensors, which are located at each wheel, or in some cases in the differential, provide this information.

Electronic Control Unit

The controller is a computer in the car. It watches the speed sensors and controls the valves.

Hydraulic Modulator

The hydraulic modulator incorporates a series of solenoid valves that can open or close the hydraulic circuits between master cylinder and the brakes. In additions, it can connect the brakes to the return pump.

The ECU monitors the wheel speed sensors at all times. It is looking for decelerations in the wheel that are out of the ordinary. It might take a car five seconds to stop from 60 mph under ideal conditions, but a wheel that locks up could stop spinning in less than a second. [10]

The ABS ECU knows that such a rapid deceleration is impossible, so it reduces the pressure to that brake until it sees an acceleration, then it increases the pressure until it sees the deceleration again. It can do this very quickly, before the tire can actually significantly change speed. The result is that the tire slows down at the same rate as the car, with the brakes keeping the tires very near the point at which they will start to lock up. This gives the system maximum braking power.

When the ABS system is in operation you will feel a pulsing in the brake pedal; this comes from the rapid opening and closing of the valves. Some ABS systems can cycle up to 15 times per second.

Electronic Stability Control

Driving safety took a big step forward in the mid-1990s when electronic stability control was introduced. The German auto supplier Bosch developed the first system, and the Mercedes-Benz S-Class and BMW 7-series were the first cars to use the new safety and regulatory devices.

It goes by many names, depending on the company. Audi calls it the Electronic Stability Program, or ESP; at Ford, it goes by Advance Trac. GM has Stabilitrak and Porsche has Porsche Stability Management. But all of these systems, no matter their names, use high-tech sensors, the cars' central computer and mechanical actions to assist in driving safely. We often read about high-performance cars having a tendency to understeer or oversteer. Understeer happens when the front wheels don't have enough traction and the car continues moving forward rather than turning.[11] Oversteer is just the opposite: the car turns farther than the driver intended causing the rear wheels to slide and the car to spin. ESC, as electronic stability control is often known, can help correct both of these situations. The components of ESP are shown as Figure 5-6.

regulatory ['rɛgjələ,torɪ]   adj.调整的

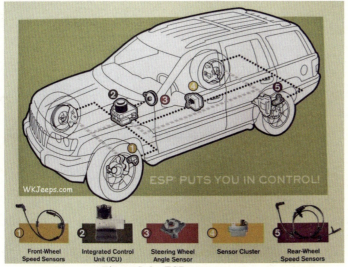

Figure 5-6 ESP components

The electronic stability control system doesn't work all alone — it uses the cars' other safety and regulatory devices, like anti-lock braking and traction control, to correct problems before they become accidents.

The center of the ESC system is also the center of the car: the yaw control sensor. Its' almost always located as close to the very center of the car as possible. If you were sitting in the drivers' seat, the yaw control sensor would be under your right elbow, somewhere between you and the passenger.

But what is "yaw"? Ships and cars both experience yaw, which is a movement around a vertical, or z, axis. The yaw sensor is located at the center of the pin. If the ESC system detects that the car is swinging too far （or not far enough） around that up-and-down axis, it takes action to assist.

Using all the modern electronic systems at its disposal, the ESC can activate one or more individual brakes, depending on which wheel can increase driving safety the most, and control the throttle to lessen the speed at which the car is traveling.[12] The sensor is looking for differences between the direction of the steering wheel and the direction the car is headed; the cars' computer then makes the necessary corrections to bring the vehicles' direction of travel in line with what the driver wanted. Figure 5-7 shows the states of the car without ESP and with ESP when it is turning.

yaw [jɔː]
n. 横摆（运动）偏航，绕垂直中轴旋转

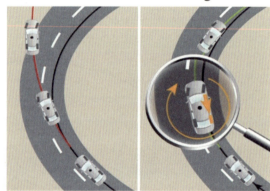

Figure 5-7　Without ESP and with ESP when turning

There are lots of safety and regulatory devices in cars these days, and they all work together to keep the wheels on the road and the passengers safe. Electronic stability control, in particular, takes advantage of two other systems, ABS and traction control, plus a few special sensors, to do its job.

Proper Names

1. ignition system　　　　　　　　　　　点火系
2. starting system　　　　　　　　　　　起动系
3. charging system　　　　　　　　　　　充电系
4. distributor　　　　　　　　　　　　　分电器

5. distributorless ignition system   无分电器式点火系统
6. spark plug   火花塞
7. one-way clutch   单向离合器
8. active safety systems   主动安全系统
9. antilock braking system (ABS)   防抱死制动系统
10. the electronic stability program (ESP)   电子稳定程序
11. hydraulic modulator   液压调节器
12. oversteer   过度转向
13. understeer   不足转向

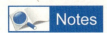 Notes

[1] It must increase battery voltage to a point where it will overcome the resistance offered by the spark plug gap and fire the plug.

翻译：它（汽车点火系统）必须增大蓄电池的电压至一定值，以克服火花塞间隙电阻并使火花塞发出火花。

[2] To make the best use of the fuel, the spark should occur before the piston reaches the top of the compression stroke, so by the time the piston starts down into its power stroke, the pressures are high enough to start producing useful work.

翻译：为了能够最大限度地利用燃油，点火应该在活塞到达压缩行程的上止点之前进行。这样的话，在活塞开始下行进入做功行程的时候，燃烧产生的压力将足够高并开始做有用功。

[3] The spark plug must have an insulated passageway for this high voltage to travel down to the electrode, where it can jump the gap and, from there, be conducted into the engine block and grounded.

翻译：为了能让高压电输送到电极，火花塞必须要有一条绝缘的通道。在火花塞的电极上，高压电使间隙之间产生跳火。电极的一端也与发动机的缸体连接并因此而搭铁。

[4] The energized coil becomes an electromagnet which pulls the plunger into the coil, the plunger closes a set of contacts which allow high current to reach the starter motor.

翻译：加电的线圈形成了一个电磁场，该电磁场将活动铁芯吸入线圈，并且接通相关电路，使强电流通到起动机。

[5] To prevent damage to the starter motor when the engine starts, the pinion gear incorporates an one-way clutch which is splined to the starter armature shaft.

翻译：为了防止起动机损坏，当发动机起动的时候，小齿轮与一个单向离合器接合，这个单向离合器通过键与起动机的转动轴连接在一起。

[6] The plunger is pulled out of contact with the battery-to-starter cables by a coil spring, and the flow of electricity is interrupted to the starter.

翻译：（当电磁场作用消失），活动铁芯在螺旋弹簧的作用下复位，断开电源与起动机的电路连接，通向起动机的电流被切断。

[7] Active safety systems help to prevent accidents and thus make a preventative contribution to road safety.

翻译：主动安全系统有助于防止事故的发生，因此它对道路交通安全做出了预防性的贡献。

[8] In fact, on slippery surfaces, even professional drivers can't stop as quickly without ABS as an average driver can with ABS.

翻译：事实上，在光滑的路面上，即便专业的驾驶员在驾驶无防抱死制动系统车辆时，也不能像一名驾驶有防抱死制动系统车辆的普通驾驶员那样，快速地使汽车停下来。

[9] A skidding wheel（where the tire contact patch is sliding relative to the road）has less traction than a non-skidding wheel.

翻译：一个拖滑抱死的车轮（轮胎与路面的接触部位相对于地面做滑动）比一个无拖滑抱死的车轮的附着力要小。

[10] It might take a car five seconds to stop from 60 mph under ideal conditions, but a wheel that locks up could stop spinning in less than a second.

翻译：在理想条件下，将一辆以时速60英里/小时行驶的轿车停下来可能需要5秒钟，但一个抱死的车轮在不到1秒钟内便可停止转动。

[11] Understeer happens when the front wheels don't have enough traction and the car continues moving forward rather than turning.

翻译：当前轮没有足够的附着力时就会发生不足转向，轿车将继续前进而不转向。

[12] Using all the modern electronic systems at its disposal, the ESC can activate one or more individual brakes, depending on which wheel can increase driving safety the most, and control the throttle to lessen the speed at which the car is traveling.

翻译：电子稳定控制系统利用了所有现代电子系统，它可以对一个或多个制动器进行控制，这取决于哪个车轮最能提高行驶安全性，也可以通过ESC控制节气门来降低车速。

Exercises

1. Choose the best answer from the following choices according to the text.

   1）_____ controls the spark and timing of the spark plug firing.

   　A. ECU　　　　B. Battery　　　　C. Ignition coil　　D. Sensor

   2）The spark plug are fired directly from the coils in a _____.

   　A. ICU　　　　　　　　B. The distributorless ignition system

   　C. engine block　　　　D. The distributor ignition system

   3）A _____ converts electrical energy into mechanical energy to rotate the engine.

   　A. alternator　　B. battery　　　C. voltage regulator　D. starter

   4）A _____ provide electricity to operate the starter.

   　A. alternator　　B. battery　　　C. engine　　　　　D. starter

   5）In a charging system, a _____ converts mechanical energy into electrical energy.

   　A. alternator　　B. battery　　　C. voltage regulator　D. starter

2. Translate the following words or phrases into Chinese.

   1）electronic ignition system　　2）Engine control unit　　3）primary current
   4）alternator　　　　　　　　　5）oversteer　　　　　　6）the charging system
   7）relay　　　　　　　　　　　8）starter　　　　　　　9）plunger

3. Translate the following words or phrases into English.

   1）火花塞　　　　　　2）点火开关　　　　　3）点火模块
   4）起动机　　　　　　5）蓄电池　　　　　　6）电压调节器
   7）电路　　　　　　　8）直流电　　　　　　9）驱动皮带

10）电子稳定程序　　　　11）电子控制单元　　12）主动安全系统

4. Translate the following sentences into Chinese.

1）The purpose of the charging system is to provide the electrical energy needed to charge the battery and to power all the electrical components and systems on the automobile.

2）The internal combustion engine must be rotated before it will run under its own power.

3）The automotive storage battery is not capable of supplying the demands of electrical system for an extended period of time. Every vehicle must be equipped with a means of replacing the current being drawn from the battery.

4）If the ABS control unit detects that one or more wheels tend to lock, it intervenes within milliseconds by modulating the braking pressure at each individual wheel.

5. Translate the words or phrases in the following figure into Chinese.

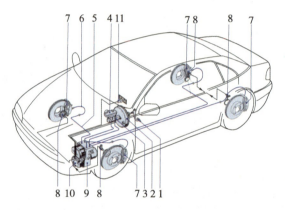

1-brake pedal; 2-brake servo unit; 3-master cylinder; 4-brake-fluid reservoir; 5-brake pipe;6-brake hose; 7-disc brake; 8-wheel speed sensor; 9-hydraulic modulator; 10-ABS control unit;11-ABS warning lamp

Practical Reading　　Anti-Lock Brake System Types

Anti-lock braking systems use different schemes depending on the type of brakes in use. We will refer to them by the number of channels — that is, how many valves that are individually controlled — and the number of wheel speed sensors.[1]

Four-channel, Four-sensor ABS

This is the best scheme. There is a wheel speed sensor on all four wheels and a separate valve for all four wheels. With this setup, the controller monitors each wheel individually to make sure it is achieving maximum braking force.

scheme [ski:m]	n. 计划, 方案
force [fɔ:s]	n. 力, 力量
effectiveness [i'fektivnis]	n. 效率, 效能, 效果, 有效性
requirement [ri'kwairmənt]	n. 必要条件, 要求

Three-channel, Three-sensor ABS

This scheme, commonly found on pickup trucks with four-wheel ABS, has a wheel speed sensor and a valve for each of the front wheels, with one valve and one sensor for both rear wheels. [2] The wheel speed sensor for the rear wheels is located in the rear axle.

This system provides individual control of the front wheels, so they can both achieve maximum braking force. The rear wheels, however, are monitored together; they both have to start to lock up before the ABS will activate on the rear. With this system, it is possible that one of the rear wheels will lock during a stop, reducing brake effectiveness.

One-channel, One-sensor ABS

This system is commonly found on pickup trucks with rear-wheel ABS. It has one valve, which controls both rear wheels, and one wheel speed sensor, located in the rear axle.

This system operates the same as the rear end of a three-channel system. The rear wheels are monitored together and they both have to start to lock up before the ABS kicks in. In this system it is also possible that one of the rear wheels will lock, reducing brake effectiveness.

This system is easy to identify. Usually there will be one brake line going through a T-fitting to both rear wheels. You can locate the speed sensor by looking for an electrical connection near the differential on the rear-axle housing.

Proper Names

1. pickup truck　　　　　　　　皮卡车
2. T-fitting　　　　　　　　　　T形接头

Notes

[1] We will refer to them by the number of channels — that is, how many valves that are individually controlled — and the number of speed sensors.

翻译：我们将根据通道和速度传感器的数量来命名（防抱死制动系统ABS的）布置方案有多少个通道就有多少个阀单独被控制。

[2] This scheme, commonly found on pickup trucks with four-wheel ABS, has a speed sensor and a valve for each of the front wheels, with one valve and one sensor for both rear wheels.

翻译：这种方案为每一个前轮设置一个车轮轮速传感器，而两个后轮则共用一个液压阀和一个传感器。该方案通常用于装备有四轮ABS的皮卡车。

学习资料

相关链接及网址：

[1] http://www.a-car.com

[2] http://www.ntis.gov.au/Default.aspx?/trainingpackage/AUR05

[3] http://www.ford.com/

推荐书目

[1] 王怡民.汽车专业英语[M].北京：人民交通出版社，2003.

[2] 马林才.汽车实用英语（下）[M].北京：人民交通出版社，2005.

[3] 陈文华.汽车发动机构造与维修[M].北京：北京航空航天大学出版社，2007.

[4] William K.Toboldt, & Larry Johnson. Automotive Encyclopedia [M]. South Holland, Illinois: The Goodheart-willcox Company, Inc，1983.

项目6　汽车车身电气设备和被动安全系统的介绍

学习目标

1. 认识关于汽车空调系统、灯光系统、中控门锁、防盗系统及被动安全系统等汽车车身电气设备的组成和工作原理的英语术语和词汇；
2. 理解汽车车身电气设备各系统常见的惯用表达方法；
3. 运用所学知识，对汽车车身电气设备的部分系统总成进行中英互译；
4. 在教师指导下，完成与汽车车身电气设备构造相关的英语资料阅读和翻译工作；
5. 正确完成课后练习。

学习时间

4学时

任务描述

介绍汽车上常见的车身电气设备元件结构及工作原理，如汽车空调系统、汽车灯光系统、安全气囊、防盗系统等。通过完成该任务，能阅读关于汽车电气设备的相关英文资料，并掌握相应内容的翻译技巧。

引导问题

你知道下图中的英文代表什么意思吗？

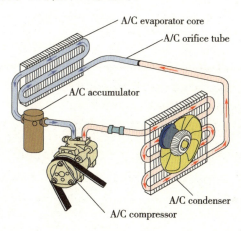

> **学习引导**
>
> 本项目的学习，应沿着以下脉络进行：
> 通读全文→学习单词和语法→完成课后练习→分组讨论→课后阅读

Project 6　Introduction to Automotive Body Electrical Equipment and Passive Safety Systems

Automotive Air Conditioning System

Air conditioning systems are designed to allow the driver and passengers to feel more comfortable during uncomfortably warm, humid, or hot trips in a vehicle. It has five basic parts: receiver dryer, expansion valve, evaporator, compressor and condenser, as shown in Figure 6-1.

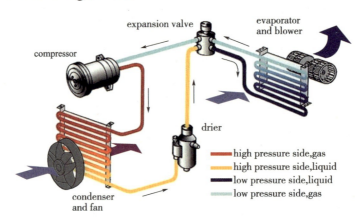

Figure 6-1　Automotive air conditioning

The Receiver Dryer（receiver）acts as a storage tank to send refrigerant to the expansion valve at all times. And another purpose is to remove moisture and filter out dirt.

Another common refrigerant regulator is the thermal expansion valve. This type of valve can sense both temperature and pressure, and is very efficient at regulating refrigerant flow to the evaporator. [1]

The evaporator provides two functions. Its primary duty is to remove heat from the inside of your vehicle. A secondary benefit is dehumidification.

As the heart of the system, the compressor is a belt driven pump that is fastened to the engine. It is responsible for compressing and transferring refrigerant gas.

The condenser is designed to radiate heat, in many cases, will have much the same appearance as the radiator in you car as the two have very similar functions. Once the refrigerant is drawn into the suction side, it is compressed and sent to the condenser, where it can then transfer the heat that is absorbed from the inside of the vehicle.[2]

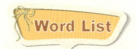

Light System

Vehicles are provided with a number of exterior lamps, including the headlamps, and these have to conform to National standards. Figure 6-2 shows the lamps at the front of a vehicle. The park lamps might be a part of the headlamp assembly, or they can be separate. The turn-signal lamps are separate and have an amber-colored lens.

The lamps for the rear of a vehicle are shown in Figure 6-3. Combination lamps are often fitted at the rear and these have more than one lamp, or are a cluster of lamps. The rear of the vehicle has stop lamps （red lens）, tail lamps （red lens）, reversing lamps （white lens） and turn-signal lamps （amber lens）. As well as these, there is the number plate lamp.

Word List

receiver[ri'si:və]　　　　　　n. 接受者，接收器
evaporator [i'væpə,retə]　　　n. 蒸发器
compressor [kəm'prɛsə]　　　n.压缩机
condenser [kən'dɛnsə]　　　　n. 冷凝器
refrigerant [ri'fridʒərənt]
　　　　　　　　　　adj.制冷的;n.制冷剂
lamp[læmp]　　　　　　　　n.灯，灯火
amber['æmbə]
　　　　　　　n.琥珀，琥珀色，黄色,黄褐色

Figure 6-2　The exterior lamps at the front of a vehicle

Figure 6-3　The exterior lamps at the rear of a vehicle

Central Locking System

Nowadays maximum people have central

Word List

alarm [ə'lɑ:m]　　　　n.警报，警报器，闹钟
siren ['saiərin]　　　　n.汽笛，警报器
joystick ['dʒɔi,stik]　　　n.操纵杆
reversible [ri'və:səbl]　adj.可反转的,可逆的
slam [slæm]　　　　vt.猛地关上，猛扔，猛推

locking system to prevent their car from theft. The central locking combination of the following two types:

★ Manual system: Power lock system allows central locking all the doors of the car including tailgate from the driver's position by pressing a button manually.

★ Remote keyless entry system: Locking and unlocking of the doors can be done by remote control as well, much in the same way that a television remote control works. By pressing a specified button on the remote, a person can enter the car without using a key.

Alarm System

Most modern car alarm systems consist of:

★ An array of sensors that can include switches, pressure sensors and motion detectors.

★ A siren, often able to create a variety of sounds so that you can pick a distinct sound for your car.

★ A radio receiver to allow wireless control from a key fob.

★ An auxiliary battery so that the alarm can operate even if the main battery gets disconnected.

★ A computer control unit that monitors everything and sounds the alarm, which is the "brain" of the system.

Power Seat

Power seats began appearing in automobiles in the late 1940s. A 6-way power seat appeared in the late 1950s. Most power seats in newer cars are either six- or eight-way. Power seat in an automobile can be adjusted by using a switch or joystick and a set of small electric motors（motor for slide, motor for up down, motor for reclining）.

In addition to fore and after adjustments, power seats can be raised or lowered and tilted to suit the comfort of the driver and/or passenger, and some cars also have memory adjustments.

Electric Rearview Mirror

A rear-view mirror is a mirror in automobiles and other vehicles, designed to allow the driver to see rearward through the vehicle's backlight. The electric rearview mirror system is composed by Lens, two small motors, circuits and control switch, and both the small motors are reversible.

Power Windows

Power windows are electric windows which can be raised and lowered at the touch of a button rather than the traditional handle which has to be turned manually for raising and lowering car windows. A simple power-window circuit is shown as Figure 6-4. When the driver presses one of the switches, one of the two side contacts is disconnected from the ground and connected to the center power contact,

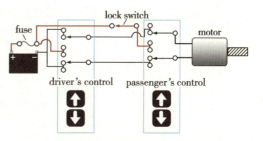

Figure 6-4 A simple power-window circuit

while the other one remains grounded. This provides power to the window motor. If the switch is pressed the other way, then power runs through the motor in the opposite direction.

Car Audio Visual Systems

The car Audio Visual Systems including multimedia, CD players, DVD players, car stereos, car speakers, car radio, subwoofers, amplifiers, MP3 players, navigation, and other car audio and DVD accessories.

Safety Belt

In crashes, people need to be retained within the occupant compartment and not be ejected, as to reduce the possible of serious injury.[3] Safety belt (seat belt) plays an important role in this. In effect, they retain you to the occupant compartment so you decelerate with it instead of slamming into hard interior surfaces. But not all belt designs are the same. Usually includes: lap belt, lap-shoulder belt, child seat [restraint] belt.

All new passenger cars have shoulder belts on inertia reels that allow upper body movement during normal driving but lock during hard braking.[4] And some has an ELR（emergency locking retractor）.

Airbag System（Supplemental Restraint System）

Even the best belt designs can't prevent all head and chest impacts in serious frontal crashes. Airbag system（Supplemental Restraint System）helps you by creating an energy-absorbing cushion between the upper body and steering wheel, instrument panel, or windshield.

The airbag system（Supplemental Restraint System）has the following equipment, is shown in Table 6-1.The components of air bag system is shown as Figure 6-5.

The airbag system equipment   Table 6-1

Item		Equipment
Frontal Collision	SRS Driver Airbag	Standard
	SRS Front Passenger Airbag	
Side/Rear Side Collision	SRS Side Airbag	Optional
	SRS Curtain Shield Airbag	
Front Passenger Occupant Classification System		Standard

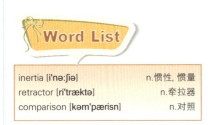

Word List

inertia [i'nə:ʃiə]   n.惯性, 惯量
retractor [ri'træktə]   n.牵拉器
comparison [kəm'pærisn]   n.对照

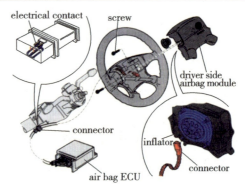

Figure 6-5　Components of an air bag system

Control Area Network（CAN）System

A vehicle can contain computerized networks designed to control all of a vehicle's functions, known as "CAN-bus" systems. As vehicle electrical systems become very complex, the CAN system can reduce wiring by up to 70 percent. Figure 6-6 is a comparison of conventional cabling and a linear BUS system.

With conventional data transfer （Figure 6-6a） every signal that is transmitted has its own conductor. The units can communicate with each other, but this requires a number of conductors for them to be able to do so. With serial data transmission （Figure 6-6 b） units with CAN interfaces can be networked. Signals can be sent and received by any of the stations, but only those signals that are needed by the particular station or stations will be accepted.

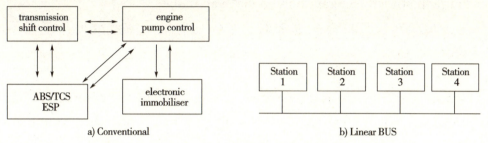

Figure 6-6　Comparison of conventional and linear BUS systems

Proper Name

1. air bag   气囊
2. expansion valve   膨胀阀
3. receiver dryer   储液干燥器
4. licence plate   牌照
5. headlamps   前照灯
6. tail lamps   尾灯
7. turn-signal lamps   转向灯
8. reversing lamps   倒车灯
9. central locking system   中控门锁
10. alarm system   报警系统，防盗系统
11. power seat   电动座椅
12. power windows   电动车窗
13. car audio visual systems   汽车视听系统
14. safety belt   安全带
15. 6-way power seat   六向电动座椅
16. motor for slide   前后调节电动机
17. motor for reclining   倾角电动机
18. lap belt   腰式安全带
19. lap-shoulder belt   腰肩式安全带
20. child seat（restraint）belt   儿童安全带
21. ELR（emergency locking retractor）紧急锁止式收紧器

22. SRS (supplemental restraint system)　　辅助约束系统
23. control area network (CAN)　　控制局域网

Notes

[1] This type of valve can sense both temperature and pressure, and is very efficient at regulating refrigerant flow to the evaporator.

翻译：这种阀门可以感知温度和压力，同时能非常有效地调节到蒸发器的制冷剂流量。

[2] Once the refrigerant is drawn into the suction side, it is compressed and sent to the condenser, where it can then transfer the heat that is absorbed from the inside of the vehicle.

翻译：一旦制冷剂从吸入端进入压缩机，它就被压缩，然后输送到冷凝器，在冷凝器中，制冷剂吸收汽车车内的热量。

[3] In crashes, people need to be retained within the occupant compartment and not be ejected, as to reduce the possible of serious injury.

翻译：在碰撞事故中，乘员应该被限制在乘员舱内而不是被抛出车外，这样可以减小受重伤的可能性。

[4] All new passenger cars have shoulder belts on inertia reels that allow upper body movement during normal driving but lock during hard braking.

翻译：所有新的乘用车都有惯性卷筒型自动安全带，它允许上半身在正常的驾驶中移动而在紧急制动时被固定住。

Exercises

1. Choose the best answer from the following choices according to the text.

　　1）_____ is the heart of the air conditioning system.
　　　　A. accumulator　　B. compressor　　C. evaporator　　D. orifice tube
　　2）Primary duty of _____ is to remove heat from the inside of your vehicle.
　　　　A. condenser　　　　　　　　B. compressor
　　　　C. evaporator　　　　　　　　D. thermal expansion valve
　　3）Most power seats in newer cars are either six- or _____-way.

A. seven   B. eight   C. nine   D. ten

4）_____ allows central locking all the doors of the car including tailgate from the driver's position by pressing a button manually.

A. central locking system   B. Power lock system
C. SRS   D. Safety belts

5）_____ which can be raised and lowered at the touch of a button rather than the traditional handle which has to be turned manually for raising and lowering car windows.

A. Power windows   B. SRS
C. ESP   D. Safety belts

2. Translate the following words or phrases into Chinese.

1）air bag   2）compressor   3）power seat
4）6-way power seat   5）accumulator   6）alarm system
7）turn-signal lamps   8）safety belt   9）tail lamps

3. Translate the following words or phrases into English.

1）冷凝器   2）安全气囊   3）压缩机
4）牌照   5）蒸发器   6）制冷剂
7）热膨胀阀   8）中控系统   9）倒车灯

4. Translate the following sentences into Chinese.

1）The rear of the vehicle has stop lamps（red lens）, tail lamps（red lens）, reversing lamps（white lens）and turn-signal lamps（amber lens）. As well as these, there is the number plate lamp.

2）Locking and unlocking of the doors can be done by remote control as well, much in the same way that a television remote control works.

3）The condenser, in many cases, will have much the same appearance as the radiator in you car as the two have very similar functions.

5. Translate the words or phrases in the following figure into Chinese.

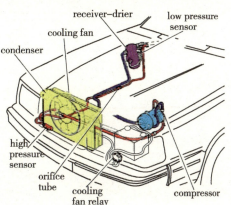

Practical Reading　Body Electronic Module（BEM）: Overview

module ['mɔdjuːl]　　　　　　n.模块
integrate ['intigreit]
　　　v t.使成一体，使结合，使合并
diagnosis [daiəg'nəusis]
　　　　　n.诊断，诊断结果，调查分析

Other sections of this volume contain references to the body electronic module（BEM）and its functions, but a brief overview will be provided here.

The body electronic module（BEM）is a centralized electronic control unit that combines the functions of a number of smaller units. Instead of having small electronic control units located at various parts of the vehicle, they are integrated into a central unit. The BEM also has a centralized self-diagnosis function. This allows electrical system faults to be accessed through a diagnosis connector.[1]

Figure 6-7 shows various components and

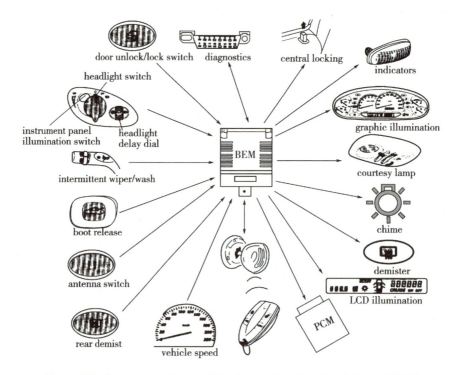

Figure 6-7　Components that send signals to and receive signals from a BEM

controls that are associated with a BEM, although the number and type will vary for different vehicles. The BEM receives input signals from various sources, processes them and then sends output signals to various components.[2] The BEM can receive signals, process signals, store and compare data, and send signals.

Proper Name

1. Body electronic module　　　车身电子模块
2. intermittent wiper　　　　　间歇式刮水器

Notes

[1] The BEM also has a centralized self-diagnosis function. This allows electrical system faults to be accessed through a diagnosis connector.

翻译：车身电子模块（BEM）具备自诊断功能。通过使用诊断连接器就能找到电路系统的问题。

[2] The BEM receives input signals from various sources, processes them and then sends output signals to various components.

翻译：车身电子模块（BEM）从各种信号源接收输入信号，处理后将输出信号输送给各部件。

学习资料

相关链接及网址：

[1] http://auto.indiamart.com/

[2] http://www.ntis.gov.au/Default.aspx?/trainingpackage/AUR05

[3] http://www.ford.com/

[4] http://en.wikipedia.org

[5] http://www.howstuffworks.com/car-alarm.htm

[6] http://www.familycar.com/ac1.htm

[7] http://automobiles.mapsofindia.com/

[8] http://auto.howstuffworks.com/

推荐书目

[1] 王怡民.汽车专业英语[M].北京：人民交通出版社，2003.

[2] 马林才.汽车实用英语（下）[M].北京：人民交通出版社，2005.

[3] 何宝文，杨雪松.汽车专业英语[M].北京：清华大学出版社，2010.

[4] William K.Toboldt, & Larry Johnson. Automotive Encyclopedia[M]. South Holland, Illinois: The Goodheart-willcox Company, Inc，1983.

项目7　新能源汽车介绍

学习目标

1. 认识新能源汽车相关的英语术语和词汇；
2. 对新能源汽车相关的资料进行简单的中英互译；
3. 对新能源汽车实物上英语单词或词汇进行辨认；
4. 认识新能源汽车构造及缩略词；
5. 阅读关于新能源汽车的英文文献，并掌握简单翻译技巧；
6. 正确完成课后练习。

学习时间

4学时

任务描述

通过介绍纯电动汽车、燃料电池汽车、油电混合动力汽车、太阳能汽车、空气动力汽车，学习各种新能源汽车的结构和原理，完成对相关词汇和语句的认识。通过完成该任务，能阅读关于新能源汽车的英文文献，并能运用所学项目知识和翻译技巧，对相关文献进行翻译。

引导问题

你知道下图中的英文代表什么意思吗？

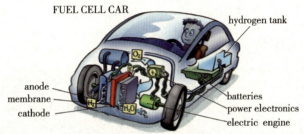

学习引导

本项目的学习，应沿着以下脉络进行：
通读全文→学习单词和语法→完成课后练习→分组讨论→课后阅读

Project 7　Introduction to the New Energy Vehicles

energy['enədʒi]
　　n.精力，精神，活力，[物]能量
battery['bætəri]　　　　　n.电池
propel[prə'pel]　　　vt.推进，驱使
significantly[sɪg'nɪfɪkəntlɪ]
　　adv.意味深长地，值得注目地，有效地
pollution[pə'luʃən]　　n.污染，沾污
potential[pə'tenʃəl]
　　adj.潜在的，可能的，势的，位的
emission[ɪ'mɪʃən]
　　n.（光、热等的）散发，发射，喷射
generate['dʒenəreit]　　vt.产生，发生
reduction[rɪ'dʌkʃən]
　　n.减少，缩影，变形，缩减量，约简
predict[pri'dikt]　　v.预知，预言，预报
decrease[di:'kri:s]
　　　　　　　n.减少，减少量；v.减少
generation[,dʒenə'reiʃən]
　　n.产生，发生，一代，一代人
fossil['fɔsl]　　adj.化石的，陈腐的，守旧的
dependence[dɪ'pendəns]
　　　　n.依靠，依赖，信任，信赖
hydrogen['haidrədʒən]　　n.氢
tailpipe['teilpaip]　　n.[汽]排气管
overcome[,əuvə'kʌm]
　　vt.战胜，克服，胜过，征服；vi.得胜
substantial[səb'stænʃəl]
　　adj.坚固的，实质的，真实的，充实的
component[kəm'pəunənt]
　　　　n.成分；adj.组成的，构成的
oxygen['ɔksidʒən]　　　n.[化]氧
storage['stɔridʒ]
　　n.储藏（量），储藏库，存储

Electric Cars

An electric car is a plug-in battery powered automobile which is propelled by electric motor(s). Electric cars have the potential of significantly reducing city pollution by having zero tail pipe emissions.[1] Vehicle greenhouse gas savings depend on how the electricity is generated. With the current U.S. energy mix, using an electric car would result in a 30% reduction in carbon dioxide emissions. Given the current energy mixes in other countries, it has been predicted that such emissions would decrease by 40% in the UK, 19% in China, and as little as 1% in Germany.

The newest generation of electric cars is a good match for the current generation of gas and/or diesel powered cars. The development is fast. With newest generation of Li-ion batteries and powerful electric motors these cars can be used for daily people and goods transports, have enough range and are faster than their fossil powered brothers. The structure of electric car is shown in Figure 7-1.

Figure 7-1　Structure of an electric car

Fuel Cell Vehicles

Fuel cell vehicles (FCVs) have the potential to significantly reduce our dependence on oil and lower harmful emissions that cause climate change. FCVs run on hydrogen gas rather than gasoline and emit no harmful tailpipe emissions. These vehicles are in the early stages of development, and several challenges must be overcome before these vehicles will be competitive with conventional vehicles. However, the potential benefits of this technology are substantial.

FCVs look like conventional vehicles from the outside, but inside they contain technologically advanced components not found on today's vehicles. The most obvious difference is the fuel cell stack that converts hydrogen gas stored onboard with oxygen from the air into electricity to drive the electric motor that propels the vehicle.[2] The major components of a typical FCV are illustrated in Figure 7-2.

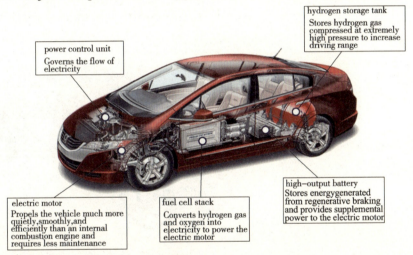

Figure 7-2　The inside look of fuel cell vehicles

Gasoline-electric Hybrid Cars

Gasoline-electric hybrid cars contain the following parts (shown as Figure 7-3):

★Gasoline engine - The hybrid car has a gasoline engine much like the one you will find on most cars. However, the engine on a hybrid is smaller and uses advanced technologies to reduce emissions and increase efficiency.

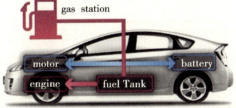

Figure 7-3　Gasoline-electric Hybrid Structure

★Fuel tank - The fuel tank in a hybrid is the energy storage device for the

Word List

sophisticate[sə'fɪs,tɪ,keɪt]
　　　　　　n.久经世故的人，多变的人
generator['dʒenəreitə]
　　　　　　　　　n.发电机，发生器
series['siəri:z]
　　　n.连续，系列，一连串，串联
accelerate[æk'seləreit]　v.加速，促进
transmission[trænz'miʃən]　n.变速器
parallel['pærəlel]
　adj.平行的，相同的，类似的，并联的
contrast['kɔntræst]
　　　　　vt.使与…对比，使与…对照
solar['səulə]　　　adj.太阳的，日光的
obtain[əb'tein]　　　　　　　v.获得

gasoline engine. Gasoline has a much higher energy density than batteries do. For example, it takes about 1,000 pounds of batteries to store as much energy as 1 gallon（7 pounds）of gasoline.

★Electric motor - The electric motor on a hybrid car is very sophisticated. Advanced electronics allow it to act as a motor as well as a generator.[3] For example, when it needs to, it can draw energy from the batteries to accelerate the car. But acting as a generator, it can slow the car down and return energy to the batteries.

★Generator - The generator is similar to an electric motor, but it acts only to produce electrical power. It is used mostly on series hybrids（shown as Figure 7-4）.

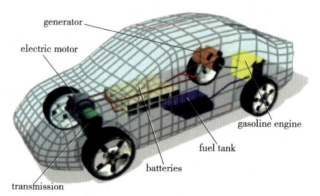

Figure 7-4　Series Hybrid Car

★Batteries - The batteries in a hybrid car are the energy storage device for the electric motor. Unlike the gasoline in the fuel tank, which can only power the gasoline engine, the electric motor on a hybrid car can put energy into the batteries as well as draw energy from them.

★Transmission - The transmission on a hybrid car performs the same basic function as the transmission on a conventional car. Some hybrids, like the Honda Insight, have conventional transmissions. Others, like the Toyota Prius, have radically different ones.

You can combine the two power sources found in a hybrid car in different ways. One way, known as a parallel hybrid , has a fuel tank that supplies gasoline to the engine and a set of batteries that supplies power to the electric motor. Both the engine and the electric motor can turn the transmission at the same time, and the transmission then turns the wheels. The Figure 7-5 shows a typical parallel hybrid.

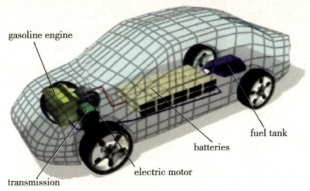

Figure 7-5　Parallel Hybrid Car

By contrast, in a series hybrid（shown as Figure 7-4）, the gasoline engine turns a generator, and the generator can either charge the batteries or power an electric motor that drives the transmission. Thus, the gasoline engine never directly powers the vehicle.Take a look at the diagram of the series hybrid, starting with the fuel tank, and you'll see that all of the components form a line that eventually connects with the transmission.

Solar Cars

A solar car is an electric car powered by solar electricity（Figure 7-6）. This is obtained from solar panels on the surface（generally, the top or window）of the car. Photovoltaic（PV）cells convert the sun's energy directly into electrical energy.

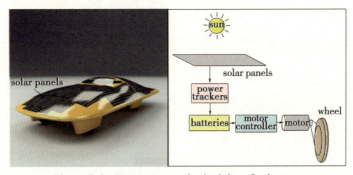

Figure 7-6　Appearance and principles of solar cars

Word List

household['haʊshəʊld]
    adj. 家庭的，家族的，家属的，普通的
industrial[ɪn'dʌstrɪəl]
    adj. 工业的，产业的，实业的，从事工业的
photon['fəʊtɒn]   n. 光子
strike[straɪk]   vt. 打，撞击，冲击
excite[ɪk'saɪt]
    vt. 刺激，使兴奋，使激动
semiconductor[ˌsemɪkən'dʌktə]
    n. [物] 半导体
silicon['sɪlɪkən]   n. [化] 硅，硅元素
alloy['ælɔɪ]
    n. 合金；vt. 使成合金，减低成色
indium['ɪndɪəm]   n. [化] 铟
gallium['gælɪəm]   n. [化] 镓
nitrogen['naɪtrədʒən]   n. [化] 氮
ethanol['eθənɔːl]   n. 乙醇，酒精

Solar cars depend on PV cells to convert sunlight into electricity. In fact, 51% of sunlight actually enters the Earth's atmosphere. Unlike solar thermal energy which converts solar energy to heat for either household purposes, industrial purposes or to be converted to electricity, PV cells directly convert sunlight into electricity. When sunlight (photons) strikes PV cells, they excite electrons and allow them to flow, creating an electrical current.[4] PV cells are made of semiconductor materials such as silicon and alloys of indium, gallium and nitrogen. Silicon is the most common material used and has an efficiency rate of 15%~20%. Of late, several consulting companies, such as Phoenix Snider Power, have started offering technical and financial services to institutes and teams developing solar cars worldwide.

Compressed Air Cars

A compressed air car is a car that uses a motor powered by compressed air. The car can be powered solely by air, or combined (as in a hybrid electric vehicle) with gasoline, diesel, ethanol, or an electric plant with regenerative braking.[5]

Compressed air cars are powered by motors fueled with compressed air, which is stored in a tank at high pressure such as 30 MPa. Rather than driving engine pistons with an ignited fuel-air mixture, compressed air cars use the expansion of compressed air, in a similar manner to the expansion of steam in a steam engine. Figure 7-7 shows the air powered car's engine.

Storage tanks are often made of carbon-fiber for weight reduction while maintaining strength; if penetrated carbon-fiber will crack but not produce shrapnel.

The principal advantages of an air powered vehicle are:

★Refueling can be done at home using an air compressor or at service stations. The energy required for compressing air is produced at large centralized plants, making it less costly and more effective to manage carbon emissions than from individual vehicles.

★Compressed air engines reduce the cost of vehicle production, because there is no need to build a cooling system, spark plugs, starter motor, or mufflers.

★The rate of self-discharge is very low opposed to batteries that deplete their charge slowly over time. Therefore, the vehicle may be left unused for longer periods of time than electric cars.

★Expansion of the compressed air lowers its temperature; this may be exploited for use as air conditioning.

★Reduction or elimination of hazardous chemicals such as gasoline or battery acids/metals

★Some mechanical configurations may allow energy recovery during braking by compressing and storing air.

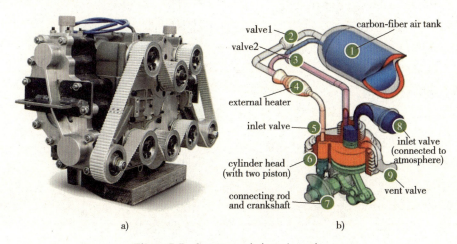

Figure 7-7 Compressed air car's engine

Compressed air cars are emission-free at the exhaust. Since a compressed air car's source of energy is usually electricity, its total environmental impact depends on how clean the source of this electricity is. Different regions can have very different sources of power, ranging from high-emission power sources such as coal to zero-emission power sources such as wind. A given region can also update its electrical power sources over time, thereby improving or worsening total emissions. However a study showed that even with very optimistic assumptions, air storage of energy is less efficient than chemical（battery）storage.

Proper Names

1.	air powered car	空气动力汽车
2.	carbon dioxide	二氧化碳
3.	carbon-fiber	碳素纤维，碳化纤维
4.	compressed air	压缩空气
5.	consulting company	咨询公司
6.	electric car	电动汽车
7.	electric motor	电动机
8.	electrical current	电流
9.	fuel cell stack	燃料电池组
10.	fuel cell vehicle	燃料电池车
11.	fuel tank	燃料罐
12.	gas-and-oxygen	汽油和氧气
13.	gasoline engine	汽油发动机
14.	gasoline-electric hybrid car	油电混合汽车
15.	greenhouse gas	温室气体
16.	harmful emission	有害排放
17.	Li-ion battery	锂离子电池
18.	parallel hybrid	并联混合
19.	photovoltaic cell	光伏电池
20.	series hybrid	串联混合
21.	solar car	太阳能汽车
22.	solar panel	太阳能板
23.	thermal energy	热能
24.	Toyota Prius	丰田普锐斯

Notes

[1] Electric cars have the potential of significantly reducing city pollution by having zero tail pipe emissions.

翻译：电动汽车没有尾气排放，具有明显减少城市污染的潜力。

[2] The most obvious difference is the fuel cell stack that converts hydrogen gas stored onboard with oxygen from the air into electricity to drive the electric motor that propels the vehicle.

翻译：最明显的不同是燃料电池组，它将车载的氢和空气中的氧转化成电流来驱动电动机，从而驱动车辆前进。

[3] Advanced electronics allow it to act as a motor as well as a generator.
翻译：先进的电子学让它同时扮演电动机和发电机两个角色。

[4] When sunlight（photons） strikes PV cells, they excite electrons and allow them to flow, creating an electrical current.
翻译：当阳光照射（光子撞击）光伏电池，光子激发电子并让其流动，从而产生一股电流。

[5] The car can be powered solely by air, or combined （as in a hybrid electric vehicle） with gasoline, diesel, ethanol, or an electric plant with regenerative braking.
翻译：这种汽车可以单独由空气驱动，或组合一台汽油、柴油、乙醇发动机或者带制动回收的电气设备（就像在一辆混合动力汽车中）。

Exercises

1. Choose the best answer from the following choices according to the text.

1）The newest generation of electric cars is a good match for the current generation of gas and/or_____powered cars.
　　A. gasoline　B. diesel　C. Liquefied Petroleum Gas　D. natural gas

2）The hybrid car has a_____engine much like the one you will find on most cars.
　　A. gasoline　　　　　　　　B. diesel
　　C. Liquefied Petroleum Gas　D. natural gas

3）A solar car is an electric car powered by_____electricity.
　　A. sun　　　B. hydrogen　　C. pure　　D. solar

4）You can combine the two power sources found in a_____car in different ways.
　　A. solar car　B. electric car　C. hybrid　D. full cell

2. Translate the following words or phrases into Chinese.

1）carbon dioxide　　2）compressed air　　3）electric motor
4）fuel cell vehicles　5）gasoline-electric hybrid car　6）harmful emission
7）Lio-Ion battery　　8）series hybrid　　9）solar car

3. Translate the following words or phrases into English.

1）并联混合　　　　2）电动汽车　　　　3）光伏电池
4）空气动力汽车　　5）汽油发动机　　　6）燃料电池组
7）太阳能板　　　　8）碳素纤维　　　　9）温室气体

4. Translate the following sentences into Chinese.

1）PV cells are made of semiconductor materials such as silicon and alloys of indium, gallium and nitrogen.

2）An electric car is a plug-in battery powered automobile which is propelled by electric motor（s）.

3）Fuel cell vehicles（FCVs）have the potential to significantly reduce our dependence on foreign oil and lower harmful emissions that cause climate change.

4）Since a compressed air car's source of energy is usually electricity, its total environmental impact depends on how clean the source of this electricity is.

5. Translate the words or phrases in the following figure into Chinese.

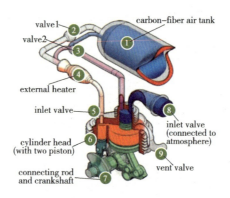

Practical Reading　New-Energy Car Strategy Proposed

cabinet['kæbɪnɪt]	n. <美>内阁
approved[ə'pru:vd]	adj.经核准的，被认可的
objective[əb'dʒektɪv]	n.目标，目的，adj.客观的
priority[praɪ'ɔrɪtɪ]	n.先，前，优先，优先权
proposal[prə'pəuzəl]	n.提议，建议

China has finished work on its automobile proposal that will become part of the 12th Five-Year Plan（2011—2015）, and new energy vehicles are a top priority, China News Service reported on Monday.

According to the plan, electric and hybrid-power vehicles will be major focuses during the five years. China is planning to become the world's biggest clean-energy car production country in future years.

Sources from the China Association of Automobile Manufacturers told the news agency that the plan will set an objective to sell 1 million clean-energy cars by 2015 in the country.[1]

Officials from the Ministry of Industry and Information Technology told the media earlier this year that the central government will invest 100 billion yuan （$15 billion） to develop clean-energy automobiles in the next 10 years, according to the report.

Xinhua News Agency reported on Monday that China's top legislature is starting to review a draft law on vehicle and vessel taxation.

The draft law describes provisions for reducing taxes on energy-saving or clean energy-powered vehicles and vessels.[2]

The State Council, China's cabinet, approved the draft on Oct 12.

Proper Names

1. Association of Automobile Manufacturers	汽车工业协会
2. clean-energy car	清洁能源汽车
3. draft law	法律草案
4. energy-saving	节约能源
5. Ministry of Industry and Information	工业和信息化部
6. State Council	国务院
7. vehicle and vessel taxation	车船税

Notes

[1] Sources from the China Association of Automobile Manufacturers told the news agency that the plan will set an objective to sell 1 million clean-energy cars by 2015 in the country.

翻译：来自中国汽车工业协会的消息称，该计划设立了到2015年在全国销售一百万辆清洁能源汽车的目标。

[2] The draft law describes provisions for reducing taxes on energy-saving or clean energy-powered vehicles and vessels.

翻译：车船税草案中表示将对能源节约和清洁能源车船进行减税。

学习资料

[1] http://en.wikipedia.org/wiki/

[2] http://www.hybridcar.com/

[3] http://www.fueleconomy.gov/feg/fuelcell.shtml

项目8　汽车性能参数及检测设备介绍

学习目标

1. 认识进口汽车上的英文标牌；
2. 认识汽车产品性能参数的相关英文词汇及相关的缩写词；
3. 运用所学知识，对汽车检测设备相关的专业术语进行中英文互译；
4. 在教师指导下，对汽车检测设备相关英文资料进行翻译；
5. 正确完成课后练习。

学习时间

6学时

任务描述

以2010款福特福克斯为例学习常见的汽车性能指标，并通过学习各种检测设备的功能原理，完成对相关单词词汇和语句的认识。通过完成该任务，能阅读关于汽车性能参数和检测设备的英文文献，并能运用所学项目知识和翻译技巧，对相关文献进行翻译。

引导问题

你知道下图中的英文代表什么意思吗？

学习引导

本项目的学习，应沿着以下脉络进行：
通读全文→学习单词和语法→完成课后练习→分组讨论→课后阅读

Project 8 Introduction to Automotive Performance Parameters and Testing Equipments

coupe['ku:peɪ]　　　　n.供两人坐的小汽车
sedan[sɪ'dæn]　　　　n.轿子，轿车，小汽车
synchronize['sɪŋkrənaɪz]　　v.同步

Automotive Performance Parameters

Let's take 2010 Ford Focus（shown in Figure 8-1）for example to introduce automotive normal performance parameters for you.

a)　　　　　　　　　　b)
Figure 8-1 2010 Ford Focus

2010 Ford Focus Overview

Small, economical, and fun, the Ford Focus is a smart choice for those looking for a compact car.

Available as a coupe or sedan the Focus includes only minor changes for 2010. The engine is a 140-hp 2.0-liter inline four-cylinder available with a five-speed manual or four-speed automatic transmission. The interior features an available SYNC system that allows the driver to synchronize mobile electronic devices such as mp3 players and cell phones. Four airbags are standard, and rear seats include headrests. Ford offers two series on the coupe, the SE and SES; and four on the sedan, the S, SE, sporty SES, and luxury SEL. New for 2010, Ford's MyKey, Message Center, anti-lock brakes, electronic stability control, remote keyless entry and power door locks are standard on all series.

The 2010 Ford Focus is a carryover from 2009.

NHTSA Frontal Crash Test

NHTSA rates crash-tested vehicles by assigning them one to five stars, with five stars indicating the most injury protection and one star indicating the least protection.

- Driver Front: ★★★★
- Passenger Front: ★★★★

2010 Ford Focus Specifications (shown as Table 8-1~Table 8-5)

Exterior of 2010 Ford Focus Table 8-1

	S 4dr Sedan	SE 4dr Sedan	SES 4dr Sedan	SEL 4dr Sedan	SE 2dr Coupe	SES 2dr Coupe
Length	175.0 "	175.0 "	175.0 "	175.0 "	175.0 "	175.0 "
Body width	67.8 "	67.8 "	67.8 "	67.8 "	67.9 "	67.9 "
Body height	58.6 "	58.6 "	58.6 "	58.6 "	58.6 "	58.6 "
Wheelbase	102.9 "	102.9 "	102.9 "	102.9 "	102.9 "	102.9 "
Curb	2,623 lbs.	2,623 lbs.	2,623 lbs.	2,623 lbs.	2,588 lbs.	2,588 lbs.

Interior of 2010 Ford Focus Table 8-2

	S 4dr Sedan	SE 4dr Sedan	SES 4dr Sedan	SEL 4dr Sedan	SE 2dr Coupe	SES 2dr Coupe
Front head room	39 "	39 "	39 "	39 "	39 "	39 "
Rear head room	38 "	38 "	38 "	38 "	38 "	38 "
Front shoulder room	53 "	53 "	53 "	53 "	54 "	54 "
Rear shoulder room	54 "	54 "	54 "	54 "	54 "	54 "
Front hip room	50 "	50 "	50 "	50 "	50 "	50 "
Rear hip room	51 "	51 "	51 "	51 "	48 "	48 "
Front leg room	41.7 "	41.7 "	41.7 "	41.7 "	41.7 "	41.7 "
Rear leg room	36.1 "	36.1 "	36.1 "	36.1 "	36.1 "	36.1 "
Luggage capacity	13.8 cu.ft.	13.8 cu.ft.	13.8 cu.ft.	13.8 cu.ft.	13.8 cu.ft.	13.8 cu.ft.
Maximum cargo capacity	13.8 cu.ft.	13.8 cu.ft.	13.8 cu.ft.	13.8 cu.ft.	13.8 cu.ft.	13.8 cu.ft.
Standard seating	5	5	5	5	5	5

Performance of 2010 Ford Focus Table 8-3

	S 4dr Sedan	SE 4dr Sedan	SES 4dr Sedan	SEL 4dr Sedan	SE 2dr Coupe	SES 2dr Coupe
Base engine size	2.0 liters	2.0 liters	2.0 liters	2.0 liters	2.0 liters	2.0 liters
Base engine type	I-4	I-4	I-4	I-4	I-4	I-4

	S 4dr Sedan	SE 4dr Sedan	SES 4dr Sedan	SEL 4dr Sedan	SE 2dr Coupe	SES 2dr Coupe
Horsepower	140 hp	140 hp	140 hp	140 hp	143 hp	143 hp
Horsepower rpm	6,000	6,000	6,000	6,000	6,000	6,000
Torque	136 lb-ft.	136 lb-ft.	136 lb-ft.	136 lb-ft.	136 lb-ft.	136 lb-ft.
Torque rpm	4,250	4,250	4,250	4,250	4,250	4,250
Drive type	front-wheel	front-wheel	front-wheel	front-wheel	front-wheel	front-wheel
Turning radius	17.1'	17.1'	17.1'	17.1'	17.1'	17.1'

Fuel of 2010 Ford Focus   Table 8-4

	S 4dr Sedan	SE 4dr Sedan	SES 4dr Sedan	SEL 4dr Sedan	SE 2dr Coupe	SES 2dr Coupe
Fuel tank capacity	13.5 gal.	13.5 gal.	13.5 gal.	13.5 gal.	13.5 gal.	13.5 gal.
EPA mileage estimates	24 City / 35 Hwy	24 City / 35 Hwy	24 City / 35 Hwy	24 City / 35 Hwy	24 City / 35 Hwy	24 City / 35 Hwy

Safety and security of 2010 Ford Focus   Table 8-5

	S 4dr Sedan	SE 4dr Sedan	SES 4dr Sedan	SEL 4dr Sedan	SE 2dr Coupe	SES 2dr Coupe
Airbags, frontal	driver and front passenger	driver and front passenger	driver and front passenger	driver and front passenger	driver and front passenger	driver and front passenger
Airbags, side impact	seat mounted, driver and passenger	seat mounted, driver and passenger	seat mounted, driver and passenger	seat mounted, driver and passenger	seat mounted, driver and passenger	seat mounted, driver and passenger
Airbags, side curtain	curtain 1st and 2nd row	curtain 1st and 2nd row	curtain 1st and 2nd row	curtain 1st and 2nd row	curtain 1st and 2nd row	curtain 1st and 2nd row
Occupancy sensor	std	std	std	std	std	std
Traction control	ABS and driveline	ABS and driveline	ABS and driveline	ABS and driveline	ABS and driveline	ABS and driveline
Height adjustable safety belts	front	front	front	front	front	front
Seatbelt pre-tensioners	front	front	front	front	front	front
Headlights	halogen	halogen	halogen	halogen	halogen	halogen
Daytime running lights	opt	opt	opt	opt	opt	opt
Illuminated entry	std	std	std	std	std	std
Remote keyless entry	keyfob (all doors)	keyfob (all doors)	keyfob (all doors)	keyfob (all doors)	keyfob (all doors)	keyfob (all doors)
Panic alarm	std	std	std	std	std	std
Door locks	power with 2 stage unlock	power with 2 stage unlock	power with 2 stage unlock	power with 2 stage unlock	power with 2 stage unlock	power with 2 stage unlock
Rear child safety door locks	std	std	std	std	NA	NA
Content theft-deterrent alarm system	NA	std	std	std	std	std
Ignition disable	SecuriLock (R)	SecuriLock (R)	SecuriLock (R)	SecuriLock (R)	SecuriLock (R)	SecuriLock (R)

Continue

	S 4dr Sedan	SE 4dr Sedan	SES 4dr Sedan	SEL 4dr Sedan	SE 2dr Coupe	SES 2dr Coupe
Theft deterrent radio	std	std	std	std	std	std
Low tire pressure warning	std	std	std	std	std	std
Panic alarm	std	std	std	std	std	std

Automobile Testing Equipment

The tune-up technician must be very familiar with and competent in the use of various forms of test equipment. With the aid of this equipment, the technician can perform two very important tasks. For instance, the test instruments when properly used quickly pinpoint malfunctions within the engine and the ignition, fuel, electrical, and emission control systems. In addition, the same equipment is an excellent quality control tool. Now, introduce common car testing equipments for you.

technician [tek'nɪʃ(ə)n] n. 技术员，技师
instrument ['ɪnstrəmənt] n. 工具，器械
pinpoint ['pɪnpɔɪnt]
 vt. 指出（原因），指示正确位置
apparatus [ˌæpəˈreɪtəs]
 n. 器械，设备，仪器

Leak Detector

Leak detector is shown in Figure 8-2. This instrument is used for locating leaks in any pressure and vacuum system, and is also used to examine the discharge troubles in electric apparatus.[1] The instrument consists of main body, ultrasonic probe, ultrasonic microphone and ultrasonic transmitter etc.

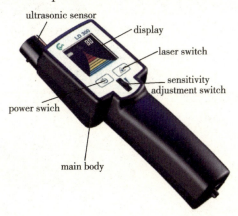

Figure 8-2 Ultrasonic leak detector

Diesel Smoke Meter

A diesel smoke meter (shown as Figure 8-3) which uses micro-waves to detect the density of black smoke contained in the exhaust gas discharged from the diesel engine through an exhaust pipe.[2] A micro-wave transmitting device is coupled to the exhaust pipe and transmits micro-waves into the exhaust pipe. Micro-waves transiting the exhaust pipe are attenuated by the black smoke in the exhaust gas. A micro-wave receiving device receives the attenuated micro-waves and provides a received signal which varies in accordance with the signal level of the attenuated micro-waves. A measuring device receives the received signal and provides an output indicative of the density of black smoke in the exhaust gas.

Figure 8-3 Diesel smoke meter

Automotive Emission Analyzer

Automotive emission analyzer is shown as Figure 8-4. This instrument is a multiplex analyzer capable of measuring 5 components in automotive emission; carbon monoxide (CO), hydrocarbon (HC), nitrogen oxides (NO_x), carbon dioxide (CO_2) and oxygen (O_2). Other than the task of measuring emission levels to determine if a vehicle's exhaust emissions comply with legal standards, the it has three other common usages. First, you can perform emission tests with this machine at various engine speeds and conditions to uncover quickly a variety of engine, ignition, and fuel-system malfunctions. Second, the analyzer provides the accuracy and range for checking and adjusting most carburetors, except those found on many vehicles with catalytic converters. Finally, the analyzer serves as a valuable quality-control tool after a tune-up to make sure that all the repair work and adjustments corrected a noted problem and restored the vehicle to manufacturer's specification.

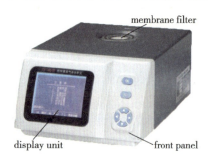

Figure 8-4 Automotive emission analyzer

Microcomputerised Engine Analyzer

Microcomputerised engine analyzer is shown as Figure 8-5. It consists of the main part, sensors and indicator. The main part is a measuring and data-handling system with a microcomputer. There are seven sensors-ignition, power supply, voltage, oil pressure, cylinder pressure, vibration and fuel injection sensors.[3]

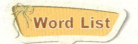

microcomputer ['maɪkrəukəmpju:tə(r)]
        n.微型计算机
readout ['redaut]   n. 读出器，读出
cradle ['kreɪdl]
    vt. 将…放在摇篮内，支持支撑

Figure 8-5　Microcomputerised engine analyzer

Chassis Dynamometer

  The chassis dynamometer（shown as Figure 8-6）is another very important diagnostic tool, found in many tune-up specialty shops. The chassis dynamometer measures the mechanical power of the vehicle at the drive-wheels and provides the operator with readout in units of road speed and power.[4] In addition, the chassis dynamometer along with an engine analyzer permits the operator to examine engine systems in detail with the vehicle operating under a loaded condition. The typical chassis dynamometer consists of two rollers, a remote control pendant, and readout instruments. The two rollers cradle the vehicle's drive wheels. One of the rollers couples directly to a power absorption unit. The power absorption unit applies a varying load on this roller upon command from the operator. The power absorption unit then acts as a very effective brake, which applies, through the roller, resistance to drive-wheel rotation. The greater the load applied by the absorption unit to the roller, the more horsepower is necessary to turn it at any given speed. Thus, at constant drive-wheel speed, the horsepower output can be made to vary by changing the load, applied by the absorption unit. Also, the operator can vary the horsepower output with a constant load applied to the drive-wheels by changing the engine speed. The remote pendant is a hand-held control used to activate the power absorption unit. The control itself has two buttons: on and off. When the technician pushes the on button in, the power absorption unit begins to load the roller. The off button, on the other hand, de-energizes the power absorption unit, thus releasing the load from the roller. The speed and power instrument panel contains two large, illuminated meters: speed and power.

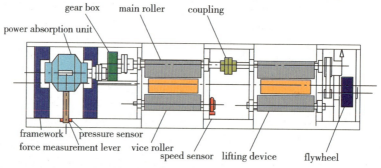

Figure 8-6 Chassis dynamometer

Automobile Side-slip Tester

This instrument (shown as Figure 8-7) is used for testing the dynamic location of the front wheels of automobile. It consists of the testing device, the quantitative indicating device and the qualitative displaying device of the sideslip.

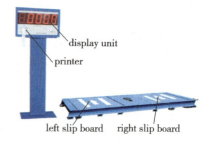

Figure 8-7 Automobile side-slip tester

Wheel Dynamic Balancer

Wheel dynamic balancer (shown as Figure 8-8) is an special equipment for conducting balancing. The electrical logging system analyses and handles signals with a single board computer. Dynamic imbalance, unlike static imbalance, can only be detected when the wheel is rotating. Dynamic balancers of the first type require the tire to be in static balance before any dynamic balancing is attempted. Dynamic imbalance can then be checked as the wheel is spun. The weights of the size indicated are placed on the wheel rim in the proper position (180° from each other on opposite wheel rims). The wheel is spun to make sure that the imbalance has been corrected. Balancers of the second type, those that combine static and dynamic balance functions, use a sensing mechanism that is sensitive to the entire weight characteristic of the tire and wheel assembly. This allows imbalance to be corrected with one weight on each side of the wheel.

Word List

pendant ['pendənt]　　　　n. 垂饰，下垂物
dynamic [dai'næmɪk]
　　　　adj. 动力的，动力学的，动态的
quantitative ['kwɒntɪtətɪv]
　　　　adj. 数量的，定量的
shield [ʃiːld]　　vt.（from）保护，防护

Figure 8-8　Wheel dynamic balancer

A wheel alignment (shown as Figure 8-9) is part of standard automobile maintenance that consists of adjusting the angles of the wheels so that they are set to the car maker's specification. The purpose of these adjustments is maximum tire life and vehicle-travel that is straight and true when driving along a straight and level road, although most machines and the technicians who use them set the alignment to adjust for crowned roads, as well as correct tracking when driving on turns.

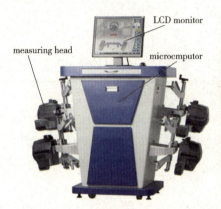 

Figure 8-9　The 4-wheel alignment gauge

speedometer[spɪ'dɒmɪtə]	n.速度表
torquemeter [tɔ:k'mɪ:tə(r)]	
	n. 转矩计，转矩测量仪

Wheel alignment can be affected by driving against a kerb, hitting a pothole in the road or by excessive wear to steering or suspension components. Alignment of wheels and tyres to the specification required by your vehicle is an important way to guarantee a smooth ride and to get the most out of your tyres.

The Wheel Alignment Systems are fitted with 4 measuring heads, 3 rotary plates and 2 rear wheel sliders. Presented with LCD monitor, these systems can operate on the temperature ranging from 1 degree Celsius to 60 degree Celsius. The computerized wheel alignment is equipped with the essential hardware such as infrared cordless remote control, sensor holders, etc. to facilitate smooth operation. These computerized wheel alignment is suited for all types of cars and is protected from unexpected data loss due to power failure.

Automobile Speedometer Tester

This equipment is used for checking the precision and the performance of automobile speedometer. It consists of the speed-test device, speed-display device and speed-alarm device.

Torquemeter

This is a torquemeter with microcomputer; it's used for measuring torque, speed and power of engine, motor and gearbox, etc.

Automobile Brake Tester

Automobile brake tester is an instrument for checking the braking performance of automobile. It consists of the actuating device, braking force supporting device, braking force detecting device and braking force indicating device. There are two types of automobile brake tester, reaction type automobile brake tester (shown as Figure 8-10) and flat automobile brake tester (shown as Figure 8-11).[5]

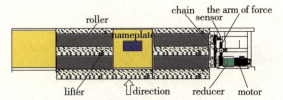

Figure 8-10　Reaction type automobile brake tester

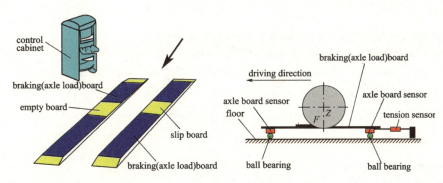

Figure 8-11　Flat automobile brake testers

Speedometer Tester

The speedometer tester is used for checking the precision and the performance of automobile speedometer. It makes up mainly of roller, lifter, measuring device, measuring instrument and auxiliary devices. Its' main structure is shown as Figure 8-12.

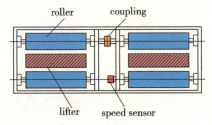

Figure 8-12　Speedometer tester

Headlight Tester

Headlight Tester is designed for testing the luminous intensity and the illuminating position (or the optical axis deviation amount) of the high / low beam of vehicle headlight. It is suitable for the vehicle testing station, auto manufacturer and vehicle repair unit to test and adjust the vehicle headlight. Its' main structure is shown as Figure 8-13.

Figure 8-13   Headlight tester

Automobile Comprehensive Tester

This instrument is used for the determination of dynamic and economic property in automobile test. It consists of main part and sensors. The main part consists of a single board computer and an interface circuit plate. Sensors include the fifth wheel sensor, fuel consumption sensor, pulling force sensor, revolution sensor and brake pedal sensor.

Performance Tester of Internal-Combustion-Engine

This is a tester for measuring the power, fuel consumption and rotational speed of engine. It consists of a microcomputer and a printing system. It is used in engine test run in combination with various dynamometers.

Proper Names

1. 4-wheel alignment gauge　　　　四轮定位仪
2. automobile brake tester　　　　汽车制动性能测试仪
3. braking performance　　　　　　制动性能
4. chassis dynamometer　　　　　　底盘测功机
5. diesel smoke meter　　　　　　　柴油机烟度计
6. drive-wheel　　　　　　　　　　驱动轮
7. engine analyzer　　　　　　　　发动机分析仪
8. engine test bed　　　　　　　　发动机试验台
9. fifth wheel sensor　　　　　　　五轮仪传感器
10. fuel consumption sensor　　　　燃油消耗传感器
11. infrared absorption analyzer　　吸收式红外分析仪
12. kingpin caster　　　　　　　　主销后倾角
13. kingpin inclination　　　　　　主销内倾角
14. leak detector　　　　　　　　　泄漏检测仪
15. performance parameter　　　　　性能参数
16. performance tester　　　　　　　性能测试仪

17. power absorption unit 动力吸收单元
18. side-slip tester 侧滑测试仪
19. single board computer 单片机
20. speedometer tester 车速表测试仪
21. ultrasonic microphone 超声波扩音器
22. ultrasonic probe 超声波探测器
23. ultrasonic transmitter 超声波讯号发送器
24. wheel camber 车轮外倾角
25. wheel dynamic balancer 车轮动态平衡机

[1] This instrument is used for locating leaks in any pressure and vacuum system, and is also used to examine the discharge troubles in electric apparatus.

翻译：该仪器用于查找所有压力和真空系统中的泄漏点，也用于查找电气设备中的漏电故障。

[2] A diesel smoke meter uses micro-waves to detect the density of black smoke contained in the exhaust gas discharged from the diesel engine through an exhaust pipe.

翻译：柴油机烟度计用微波来检测柴油机排气管中所排出的废气中黑烟的浓度。

[3] There are seven sensors-ignition, power supply, voltage, oil pressure, cylinder pressure, vibration and fuel injection sensors.

翻译：发动机分析仪上有七种传感器，分别是点火传感器、电源供给传感器、电压传感器、油压传感器、汽缸压力传感器、振动传感器和燃油喷射传感器。

[4] The chassis dynamometer measures the mechanical power of the vehicle at the drive-wheels and provides the operator with a readout in units of road speed and power.

翻译：底盘测功机能测量车辆驱动轮上的机械功率，并能向操作员显示车辆行驶速度和功率的具体读数。

[5] There are two types of automobile brake tester, reaction type automobile brake tester and flat automobile brake tester.

翻译：有两种汽车制动试验装置：反力式汽车制动试验台和平板式汽车制动试验台。

Exercises

1.Choose the best answer from the following choices according to the text.

1）Diesel Smoke Meter is used for the measurement of smoke emitted from vehicle with_____engine.

  A. gasoline   B. diesel

  C. Liquefied Petroleum Gas   D. natural gas

2）If the engine does not burn up all the fuel during the combustion process, raw gasoline goes out the tailpipe and registers as_____on the meter.

  A. CO   B.CO_2 C. NO_x D. HC

3）The typical chassis dynamometer consists of_____rollers, a remote control pendant, and readout instruments.

  A. two   B. three   C. four   D. five

4）The weights of the size indicated are placed on the wheel rim in the proper position（_____from each other on opposite wheel rims）.

  A. 90°   B. 120°   C. 180°   D. 270°

2.Translate the following words or phrases into Chinese.

  1）microcomputer   2）technician   3）speedometer

  4）kingpin inclination   5）wheel camber   6）opacimeter

  7）fuel consumption   8）leak detector   9）power absorption unit

3. Translate the following words or phrases into English.

  1）柴油机烟度计   2）底盘测功机   3）发动机试验台

  4）四轮定位仪   5）发动机分析仪   6）侧滑测试仪

  7）五轮仪传感器   8）单片机   9）车轮动平衡仪

4. Translate the following sentences into Chinese.

1）The infrared analyzer is a device that measures the amount of hydrocarbons（HC）and carbon monoxide（CO）in a vehicle's exhaust.

2）This instrument is used for testing the dynamic location of the front wheels of au tomobile.

3）This is a torquemeter with microcomputer, it's used in measuring torque, speed and power of engine, motor and gearbox, etc.

4）This instrument is for testing and correcting the bending and torsion of connecting rod.

5. Translate the words or phrases in the following figure into Chinese.

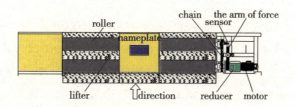

Practical Reading　Engine Noise Diagnosis

The ability to diagnose engine noises with a fair degree of accuracy may be a vital part of the tune-up specialist's job. For instance, it may be necessary for a technician to recognize and locate the cause of noises that may develop due to normal engine wear and tear over long periods of use or may appear because of failure of one or more engine parts. The parts that produce some characteristic noises are loose pistons, excessively worn rings or ring lands, loose piston pins, worn connecting-rod bearings, worn main bearings, loose vibration damper or flywheel, or worn or loose valve-train components.[1] When properly interpreted, these noises are a definite aid in any diagnosis of engine mechanical difficulties. But there are many sources and varieties of engine noises; careful interpretation of these sounds is necessary for several reasons. First, a careful diagnosis of an engine noise can often prevent the expense of tearing down an engine. In this regard, a technician should always make a noise analysis before engine repair begins so that only the needed and correct operations are made with no extra work or charges to the customer. Second, a careful interpretation of abnormal engine sounds can prevent the engine from requiring extensive and costly repair work after continued usage has ruined it.[2]

🔍 Stethoscope

All moving mechanical engine parts create some form of sound waves of various pitches, frequencies, qualities, and intensities. Most people can hear many of these sound waves without the assistance of a listening device. On the other hand, some sounds are impossible to hear unless magnifies; even if some sounds are audible, they

diagnose['daiəgnəuz]　　　　　v. 诊断
vital['vaitəl]　　　adj. 重大的，至关重要的
definite['definit]　　　adj. 明确的，一定的
expense[iks'pens]　　　　n. 费用，代价
customer['kʌstəmə]　　　　　　n. 消费者
ruin['ruin]　　　　　　　　v.（使）毁灭

are frequently difficult to localize and locate. Consequently, most technicians utilize some form of sounding rod or stethoscope when diagnosing engine sounds. A stethoscope, or sound scope, aids in locating the source of engine knocks and noises by magnifying their sound waves. This instrument makes use of a metal prod, about 8 inches long and 1/8 inch in diameter, that passes through a rubber bushing and terminates against a metal diaphragm held in a plastic housing. Furthermore, two ear tubes carry the sound from this diaphragm chamber to the listener's ears. The value of the sound-detecting and amplifying stethoscope is, of course, to help the technician distinguish the difference between normal and abnormal sounds and to find the location and cause of the latter.[3] Even an engine in good operating condition will make noises that the mechanic will be able to hear with a stethoscope. Being familiar with these sounds will be very helpful when the mechanic attempts to pinpoint the location and cause of any abnormal noise due to excessive wear, damage, or maladjustment of engine parts.

Sound tracing with the stethoscope

The best way to trace any type of noise is to follow a systematic procedure. First, for example, always use a stethoscope or other sounding device to amplify the sound. Second, with the listening device, attempt to localize and identify the noise. You can trace both unfamiliar and familiar sounds to the portion of the engine where they originate by following the sound with the prod of the stethoscope until the noise reaches its maximum intensity.[4] After you locate this spot, a knowledge of engine construction and operation will be your best guide as to the most likely cause of the sound.

Word List

stethoscope['steθəskəup]　　　　n. 听诊器
pitch[pitʃ]　　　　　　　　　　n. 程度
audible['ɔːdəbl]　　　　　　adj. 听得见的
localize['ləukəlaɪz]　　vt. 使局限于某一地方
distinguish[dɪ'tɪŋgwɪʃ]　　　v. 区别，辨别
maladjustment['mælə'dʒʌstmənt]
　　　　　　　　　　　　n. 失调，不适应
originate[ə'rɪdʒɪneɪt]　　　vt. 引起，发生
intensity[ɪn'tensiti]　　　　　　n. 强度

Proper Names

1. makes use of　　　　　　　　　使用，利用
2. rubber bushing　　　　　　　　橡胶套管

3. engine knock　　　　　　　　　　　　发动机爆震
4. metal diaphragm　　　　　　　　　　金属膜片

[1] The parts that produce some characteristic noises are loose pistons, excessively worn rings or ring lands, loose piston pins, worn connecting-rod bearings, worn main bearings, loose vibration damper or flywheel, or worn or loose valve-train components.

翻译：产生一些特别噪声的部件有松动的活塞、过度磨损的活塞环或环岸、松动的活塞销、磨损的连杆轴承、磨损的主轴承、松动的减振器或飞轮以及磨损或松动的配气机构的元件等。

[2] Second, a careful interpretation of abnormal engine sounds can prevent the engine from requiring extensive and costly repair work after continued usage has ruined it.

翻译：第二，对发动机异常噪声的正确解读能避免因继续使用而导致发动机损坏后，而付出大量维修工作和昂贵的维修费用。

[3] The value of the sound-detecting and amplifying stethoscope is, of course, to help the technician distinguish the difference between normal and abnormal sounds and to find the location and cause of the latter.

翻译：探测和放大声音的听诊器用途（价值）在于帮助，技师辨别发动机内的正常声音和异常声音，并确定发出异常声音的部位和原因。

[4] You can trace both unfamiliar and familiar sounds to the portion of the engine where they originate by following the sound with the prod of the stethoscope until the noise reaches its maximum intensity.

翻译：你可以跟踪那些熟悉或不熟悉的噪声找到发动机上噪声源，用听诊器指针在发动机上跟踪噪声，噪声最大的部位便是噪声源。

学习资料

[1] http://en.wikipedia.org/wiki/Automatic_test_equipment
[2] http://www.directindustry.com/industrial-manufacturer/leak-detector-66297.html
[3] http://www.autoacsystems.com/_faqs/detail/headline_leakdetect.html
[4] http://www.exhaust-gas-analyzer.com/

汽车实用英语

项目9　汽车故障诊断仪和数据流

学习目标

1. 熟悉典型汽车故障诊断仪数据流名称的英文表达；
2. 熟悉典型汽车故障诊断仪数据单位的英文表达；
3. 熟悉汽车故障诊断仪英文菜单界面的英文表达；
4. 正确完成课后练习。

学习时间

4学时

任务描述

通过介绍故障诊断仪的结构和操作方法，完成对相关词汇和语句的认识。通过完成该任务，熟悉故障诊断仪的英文界面操作方法，并能运用故障诊断仪进行车辆的故障诊断。

引导问题

你知道下图中仪器的作用是什么，如何操作该仪器吗？

学习引导

本项目的学习，应沿着以下脉络进行：
通读全文→学习单词和语法→完成课后练习→分组讨论→课后阅读

Project 9　Introduction to the Diagnostic Tester and Data Flow

V.A.G1552 Vehicle System Tester Features (shown as figure.9-1)

The V.A.G1552 Vehicle system tester is an easy-to-use test instrument. Take a moment to familiarize yourself with the tester features.

Word List

diagnostic [,daɪəg'nɒstɪk]
　　　　adj.诊断的，n.诊断程序,症状,诊器
socket ['sɒkɪt]
　　　　n.插座，插口，vt.装上或插入插座

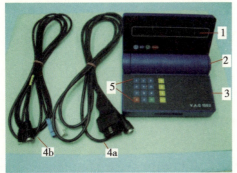

Figure 9-1　Tester and diagnostic cables

1.Display: Here you can read off the data which the unit outputs.

2.Socket for connecting diagnostic cable（the diagnostic cable is the connection cable between tester and vehicle）.

3.Covers for program card and the RS 422 interface.

4.Diagnostic cables

4a. V.A.G. 1551/3 for vehicles with 16-pin diagnostic connection

4b. V.A.G. 1551/1 for vehicles with 2-pin diagnostic connection

5.Keyboards

0 to 9 Keys for numerical entries

　C　You can use this key to erase entries, return to the previous operating level or to interrupt a program in operation

　Q　You can use this key to perform（confirm）entries

　→　You can use this key to move forward within the program or the text

　↑ and ↓　You can use these keys to change the adaptation values in function 10"Adaptation"or can run through the measuring value blocks in function 04 "Basic setting"

and in function 08 "Read measuring value block".

HELP You can retrieve additional operating information by pressing the HELP key.

How can you operate the tester?

Changing the Program Card

All the functions of the tester are controlled by the software of the program card. The program card is the size of a cheque card.

When new vehicles come onto the market, the software for the tester has to be updated. The program card then has to be changed.

> Caution! You must not remove or insert the program card unless the power has been switched off, in other words when the diagnostic cable is not connected to the vehicle! Please do not touch the contacts of the program card! And please also avoid static charges!

Please perform the following steps to change the program card:

(1) Remove the cover for the slot of the program card on the right-hand side of the housing (shown as Figure 9-1, number 3). Slacken the Phillips screw for this purpose!

(2) Take hold of the tab on the sticker and pull the card out to the right.

(3) Insert the new program card into the slot as far as it will go. Please ensure that you insert the card properly-this is illustrated on the sticker.

(4) Now, push the tab of the sticker in and up and close the cover of the slot.

(5) Switch on the power supply of the tester.

(6) Select operating mode 3. The tester starts by performing a self-test.

If the self-test is completed without any fault, the old program card is no longer needed.

Connecting the Tester

The tester is equipped with a reverse polarity protection for the power supply through the diagnostic cable.[1] Nevertheless, the input and output stages of the tester are only reliably protected if the diagnostic cable is correctly connected.

For this reason, when connecting the diagnostic cable V.A.G. 1551/1 and also diagnostic cable V.A.G. 1551/3, always keep to a certain sequence as follows:

Word List

adaptation [ˌædæpˈteɪʃən]
　　　　　　　　n.适应，改写（本）
slot [slɔt]　　n.狭缝，槽；v.插入，放置
slacken [ˈslækən]　vt.放松，减缓，减弱
screw [skruː]
　　n.螺丝（钉）；vt.用螺钉固定，拧，拧紧

(1) With the diagnostic cable V.A.G. 1551/1 (with fault finding):

①Plug the black connector for the power supply of the diagnosis tester into the black flat-contact socket in the vehicle.

②Pay attention to the readout in the display. The following text must be displayed:

> Vehicle system test   HELP
> Enter address word XX

Once the text appears in the display, plug in the white connector. If this readout does not appear in the display, do not plug in the white connector! Either the polarity of the power supply to the tester is reversed or there is no power.

③Check the voltage at the black flat-contact socket in the vehicle (see letter A in Figure 9-2) and pay attention to the polarity to avoid incorrect polarity![2] The power supply must be at least 10 volts (re-charge the vehicle battery, if necessary!).

④Test the diagnostic cable V.A.G. 1551/1 for continuity as shown in Figure 9-3.

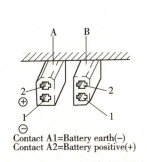

Figure 9-2 Connections on vehicle for power supply (A) and diagnosis (B)

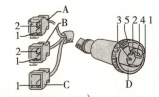

a)

At vehicle		At tester
Flat-contact connector	contact	Connector-Dcontact
black-A-	1	3 Battery(-)
	2	2 Battery(+)
white-B-	1	4 L wire
	2	1 K wire
blue-C-	1	5 Lamp lead

b)

Figure 9-3 Diagnostic cable V.A.G 1551/1

(2) With the diagnostic cable V.A.G.1551/3 (with fault finding):

①Plug the diagnostic cable into the diagnosis connection in the vehicle.

②Pay attention to the readout in the display. The following text must be displayed:

> Vehicle system test   HELP
> Enter address word XX

If this readout does not appear in the display, check the voltage at the diagnosis connection in the vehicle according to Figure 9-4 and pay attention to the polarity.

The power supply must be at least 10 volts (recharge the vehicle battery, if necessary!)

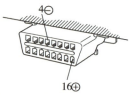

Contact 4=Battery earth(−)
Contact 16=Battery positive(+)

Figure 9-4　Connection on vehicle for diagnosis

③Test the diagnostic cable V.A.G. 1551/3 for continuity as shown in Figure 9-5.

At Vehicle Contact	At tester Connector–D–/Contact
4	3 Battery(−)
7	1 K wire
14	5 Lamp lead
15	4 L wire
16	2 Battery(+)

b)

Figure 9-5　Diagnostic cable V.A.G. 1551/3

If no readout appears in the display, this may also be caused by a soiled program card. In this case, clean the contacts of the program card with a lint-free cloth soaked in methylated spirits and re-insert the card in the slot.[3]

(3) The operating modes which you can select

Important preliminary remarks: The texts which you see in these operating instructions in the display are only examples. The texts which actually appear depend on the control unit which is connected and on the program card version used. If you operate with different systems, you must also use the relevant workshop manuals.

Word List

methylated ['meθileitid]　　adj. 加入甲醇的
dealership ['di:ləʃip]
　　　　　　　　n. 代理权，经销权，代理商
interrogate [in'terə,geit]　　　　　　v. 查询
alter ['ɔ:ltə]　　　　　　v. 改变，改动，变更

Once you have connected the tester, you can select three different operating modes:

①Operating mode 1 （"Vehicle System Test"）

②Operating mode 3 （"self-test"）

③Operating mode 4 （"dealership number"）

After the tester has been connected, it automatically moves into operating mode 1 （"Vehicle System Test"）. In other words:

> Vehicle System Test　　　　　　HELP
> Enter address word XX

You can select operating modes 3 and 4 by pressing the key C. The following text then appears in the display:

> 1-Vehicle System Test　　　　　HELP
> 3-Self-test　　　　　　4-Dealership number

If you press the HELP key, operating information appears on the display.

> Vehicle System Test　　　　　　HELP
> Enter address word XX

If this operating mode is selected after connecting the tester, please first of all enter two digits with the keyboard. These digits are the address word of the control unit. This address word is used to select the individual control units in the vehicle.

If you press the HELP key, the list of address words appears in the display （shown as Table 9-1）:

The list of address words　　　　　　　　　　　　　　　Table 9-1

Address word	Designation of system	Address word	Designation of system
01	Engine electronics	24	Drive slip control
41	Diesel pump electronic	15	Airbag
02	Gearbox electronics	26	Electronic roof control
12	Clutch electronics	17	Dash panel insert
03	Brake electronics	08	AC/Heating electronics
14	Wheel damping electronics	00	Automatic test sequence
（interrogate and display fault memory for all systems）			

After entering the address word （for example"01"） and pressing the key Q, the address word and the designation of the system are displayed in the second line of the display.

> Vehicle System Test   Q
> 01-Engine electronics

You can still alter the entry with the key C.

The address word 00 represents a special case. You can use this address word to start an automatic test sequence:

> Vehicle System Test   Q
> 00-Automatic test sequence

If you press the key Q, the tester sends the entire known address words one after the other. If a control unit answers with its control unit identification, this appears in the display. The tester now reads the fault memory. The faults recognized appear automatically in the display one after the other. After the contents of fault memory have been output, the dialogue with the control unit is ended and the next address word is sent.

Note: If no dialogue takes place with a control unit （because of an open circuit in the wiring to this control unit or control unit is faulty）, this control unit does not appear in the display.

Once the tester has sent the last address word or the contents of the last fault memory have been read, it switches to the initial operating level.[4]

How is the datalink to a control unit established?

Enter the address word （e.g. "01"）. The following text appears in the display:

> Vehicle System Test   Q
> 01-Engine electronics

If you now press the key Q, the tester establishes the datalink to the control unit. The following text appears in the display:

| digit ['dɪdʒɪt] | n. 数字，位数 |

> Vehicle System Test   Q
> Tester sends address word 01

The control unit now answers with its control unit identification:

> 0123456789 ENGINE   →
> Coding 00012   WSC 01234

If you now press the → key, you can select the individual functions:

> Vehicle System Test   HELP
> Select function XX

If you press the key, the tester displays a list of the functions which you can select（shown as Table 9-2）:

A list of functions   Table 9-2

01 –	Interrogate control unit version
02 –	Interrogate fault memory
03 –	Final control diagnosis
04 –	Basic setting
05 –	Erase fault memory
06 –	End output
07 –	Code control unit
08 –	Read measuring value block
09 –	Read individual measuring value
10 –	Adaptation

If you wish to select one of these functions, please enter one of the two-digit numbers and confirm this entry with the key Q. The tester then sends a command to the control unit. If no provision is made for the selected function in the control unit or if the command cannot be performed because of the present operating state, the following text will appear in the display:

> Function is unknown or cannot be   →
> carried out at the moment.

🔍 Normal Engine Data Flow

Enter the address word 08, press the key Q, the following text appears in the display:

> Read measuring Value block   HELP
> Enter display group number ××

If necessary, enter the group number, you can read the AFE engine data flow, the meaning of each category as follows（shown as Table 9-3）.

The meaning of each category   Table 9-3

Group number	meaning
01	Basic function, system status
02	Basic function, intake air temperature signal
03	Basic function, throttle signal
04	Basic function, speed signal
05	Basic function, Carbon tank signal

The normal range of AFE engine's data flow signals（idle）is in the Table 9-4.

The normal range of AFE engine's data flow signals   Table 9-4

Display group number	Screen display	Parameters	Normal data（idle）
01	Read measuring Value block 01 1 2 3 4	1-engine speed	800 ± 30r/min
		2-cooling water temperature	80~105℃
		3-λ sensor voltage	0~1.5V
		4-system status	00100000
02	Read measuring Value block 02 1 2 3 4	1-engine speed	800 ± 30r/min
		2-engine load	1.0~2.5ms
		3-system voltage	10.0~14.5V
		4-intake air temperature	Vary with ambient temperature
03	Read measuring Value block 03 1 2 3 4	1-engine speed	800 ± 30r/min
		2-engine load	1.0~2.5ms
		3-throttle angle	0~5°
		4-	-
04	Read measuring Value block 04 1 2 3 4	1-engine speed	800 ± 30r/min
		2-engine load	1.0~2.5ms
		3-vehicle speed	0
		4-engine status	01000001
05	Read measuring Value block 05 1 2 3 4	1-engine speed	800 ± 30r/min
		2-carbon canister clear	TE not active
		3-	-
		4-	-

Proper Names

1. reverse polarity — 反接，反极性接法，逆极性
2. flat-contact socket — 扁平插座
3. plug in — 给…接通电源，连接
4. flat-contact connector — 扁平连接器
5. engine electronics — 发动机电子控制系统
6. diesel pump electronic — 柴油泵电子控制系统
7. gearbox electronics — 变速器电子控制系统
8. clutch electronics — 离合器电子控制系统
9. brake electronics — 制动器电子控制系统
10. wheel damping electronics — 车轮阻尼电子控制系统
11. drive slip control — 驱动防滑控制
12. electronic roof control — 电子车顶控制
13. dash panel insert — 仪表盘插件
14. AC/Heating electronics — 空调/暖风电子控制系统
15. interrogate fault memory — 查询故障储存内容
16. sensor voltage — 传感器电压
17. engine load — 发动机负荷
18. engine status — 发动机状态
19. intake air temperature — 进气温度

Notes

[1] The tester is equipped with a reverse polarity protection for the power supply through the diagnostic cable.

翻译：该测试仪装备有极性保护装置，以便通过测试电缆提供电源。

[2] Check the voltage at the black flat-contact socket in the vehicle (see letter A in Figure 9-2) and pay attention to the polarity to avoid incorrect polarity!

翻译：检测车辆上黑色扁插头插座上的电压（见图9-2中的字母A），注意极性，防止极性接错！

[3] In this case, clean the contacts of the program card with a lint-free cloth soaked in methylated spirits and re-insert the card in the slot.

翻译：在这种情况下，用不起毛的甲基化酒精浸湿的布清洁程序卡的接触处，并重新插入卡插槽。

[4] Once the tester has sent the last address word or the contents of the last fault memory have been read, it switches to the initial operating level.

翻译：一旦测试仪送出最后一个地址字符或最后的故障存储内容已读出，它就切换到初始操作级。

Exercises

1. Choose the best answer from the following choices according to the text.

1）If you wish to select one of these functions, please enter one of the _____numbers and confirm this entry with the key Q.

A. one-digit　　B. two-digit　　C. one digit　　D. two digits

2）The texts which actually appear_____the control unit which is connected and on the program card version used.

A. depend on　　B. depends on　　C. dep　　D. depended

3）_____the diagnostic cable into the diagnosis connection in the vehicle.

A. Plug　　B. Take　　C. Make　　D. Send

4）You must not remove or insert the program card_____the power has been switched off.

A. when　　B. after　　C. unless　　D. which

2. Translate the following words or phrases into Chinese.

1）reverse polarity　　　　2）flat-contact socket
3）engine electronics　　　4）diesel pump electronic
5）brake electronics　　　 6）airbag
7）fault memory　　　　　8）wheel damping electronics
9）AC/Heating electronics

3. Translate the following words or phrases into English.

1）故障诊断仪　　2）故障存储器　　3）负极
4）操作模式　　　5）扁平插座　　　6）变速器电控系统
7）安全气囊　　　8）组合仪表　　　9）电动车顶控制

4. Translate the following sentences into Chinese.

1）When new vehicles come onto the market, the software for the tester has to be updated. The program card then has to be changed.

2）You must not remove or insert the program card unless the power has been switched off, in other words when the diagnostic cable is not connected to the vehicle!

3）If the self-test is completed without any fault, the old program card is no longer needed.

4）If you now press the key Q, the tester establishes the datalink to the control unit.

5. Translate the words or phrases in the following figure into Chinese.

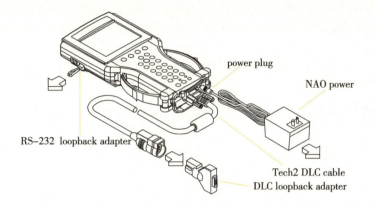

Practical Reading Passat K Line Fault Diagnosis Cases

A 2003 car models of the Passat 1.8GLS ABS fault lights lit. VAG1552 testing, elected by good ABS control unit 03, press Q, address key is confirmed, instrument shows: "K wire not switching to positive", and explain VAG1552 and ABS control unit cannot build communication. Later on other systems for testing, found that all systems appear same circumstance, cannot detect.

Failure analysis :" K wire not switching to positive" means the K line you cannot convert to the positive,[1] K line of short circuit or a control unit of K line interface, resulting in damage grounding to communication. Open the ignition switch, using

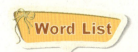

communication [kə,mju:ni'keiʃən]
　　n.交流，通信；[pl.]通信（或交通）工具
interface ['intəfeis]　n.接口；界面，交接处
multimeter [,mʌlti'mi:tə]
　　　　　　　n. 万用表; vt 多点测量
preliminary [pri'liminəri]
　　　　　a.预备的，初步的 ;n.[pl.] 初步做法
coexist ['kəuig'zist]
　　　vi. 同时存在（于同一处），共存
simultaneously [saiməl'teiniəsli]
　　　　　　　　　　　ad.同时，一起

a multimeter to check K line voltage, voltage for leel V or so, detection of K line resistance of 0.5 Ω around. Preliminary can judge, this is due to K line to short-circuit caused diagnostic instrument with auto control unit cannot communications.[2]

Check 2003 GLS diagram of Passat 1.8, analysis the diagnosis of interface circuit. This car K line and CAN – BUS line coexist. Including air conditioning control unit, radio, comfortable system central control unit through K line carries on the diagnosis and communications, ABS control unit, airbag control unit, automatic transmission control unit, engine control unit and meter control unit used simultaneously K line and the CAN-BUS line – carries on the diagnosis and communications.

Proper Names

1. failure analysis   故障分析
2. airbag control unit   安全气囊控制单元

Notes

[1] Failure analysis: "K wire not switching to positive" means the K line you cannot convert to the positive.

翻译：故障分析：" K wire not switching to positive" 的含义是K线与正极断路。

[2] Preliminary can judge, this is due to K line to short-circuit caused diagnostic instrument with auto control unit cannot communications.

翻译：初步判断，这是由于K线短路引起的汽车控制单元不能与诊断仪器通信。

学习资料

[1] http://en.wikipedia.org/wiki/Diagnostic_test
[2] http://www.obdchina.com/

项目10　汽车使用说明书及维修资料

学习目标

1. 掌握使用汽车专业词典阅读与翻译汽车英文资料的方法；
2. 掌握汽车英文资料中专业术语；
3. 熟悉汽车英文资料中常见的英文词汇与缩写；
4. 阅读汽车英文使用说明书及维修资料，并掌握基本翻译技巧；
5. 正确完成课后练习。

学习时间

6学时

任务描述

以BMW730d为例学习英文的汽车使用说明书，学习转向盘和仪表盘上各种按钮及指示灯的含义，学习仪表盘上的不同颜色指示灯所代表的故障含义；以Lexus为例，学习识读电路图和继电器的安装位置，完成对相关单词词汇和语句的认识。通过完成该任务，能阅读关于汽车使用说明书的英文文献，并能运用所学项目知识和翻译技巧，对相关维修资料进行翻译。

引导问题

你知道下图的仪表灯亮代表什么意思吗？

学习引导

本项目的学习，应沿着以下脉络进行：
通读全文→学习单词和语法→完成课后练习→分组讨论→课后阅读

Project 10　Car Manual and Maintenance Information

acquaint [ə'kweint]
　　vt.（with）使认识，使了解，使熟悉
interactive [,intə'æktiv]
　　　　　　　adj.相互作用的,交互的
derive [di'raiv]
　　　　　　vt.取得；追溯起源；
　　　　　　vi.（from）起源，衍生
resale [,ri:,seil]　　　n. 再贩卖, 转售
lane [lein]　　　　　n.（乡间）小路
　　（巷），车（跑，泳）道，航道
indicator ['indikeitə]　n.指示者，指示物
horn [hɔ:n]　　　　　n.喇叭，警报器

Car Manual （Owner's Handbook for Vehicle）

This manual is for BMW 730d, 740i, 740Li, 750i and 750Li. Firstly, congratulations on your choice of a BMW. The better you are acquainted with your car, the easer you will find it is to handle. We would therefore like to offer you the following advice:

Please read the owner's handbook before setting out in your new BMW. Also use the interactive Owner's handbook in your vehicle. It contains important notes on how to operate the car, enabling you to derive maximum benefit from the technical advantages of your BMW. It also contains useful information which will help you to uphold both the car's operating safety and its full resale value.[1]

Around the Steering Wheel

The following describes the operation buttons around the steering wheel （shown as Figure 10-1）.

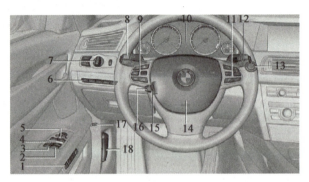

Figure 10-1　Operation buttons around the steering wheel

1. Seat comfort function

   [icon] Gentleman function

   [icon] Seat, minor, steering wheel memory

   [icon] Active seat

2. Roller sunblind for rear window
3. Safety switch for windows and roller sunblind in the rear
4. Power windows
5. Exterior mirror operation
6. Drive assistance systems

   [icon] Lane departure warning

   [icon] Forward alert

   [icon] Lane deviation warning

   [icon] Night vision with person recognition

   [icon] Head-up display

7. Lights

   [icon] Front fog lights

   [icon] Rear fog lights

   [icon] Side lights

   [icon] Low-beam-dipped-headlights

   [icon] Automatic driving lights control
       Daytime driving lights
       Adaptive headlights
       High-beam assistant

   [icon] Instrument lighting

8. Steering-column lever, left

   [icon] Flashing turn in indicators

   [icon] High-beam headlights, headlight flasher

   [icon] High-beam assistant

   [icon] Parking lights

   [icon] Onboard computer

9. Buttons on steering wheel, left

   [SET] Memorising the speed

   [PES] Calling up the speed

   [I/O] System on/off, interrupting

   [icon] Increasing the distance

   [icon] Reducing the distance

10. Instrument cluster
11. Buttons on steering wheel, right

    [MODE] Entertainment source

    [icon] Volume control

    [icon] Voice control

    [icon] Telephone

12. Steering-column lever, right

    [icon] Windscreen wipers

    [icon] Rain sensor

    [icon] Cleaning the windows and headlights

13. [START STOP ENGINE] Switching the ignition on/off and starting/stopping the engine
14. Horn

    [icon] Steering wheel heating

15.
16. [icon] Steering wheel adjustment
17. [icon] Opening luggage compartment lid
18. Unlocking luggage compartment lid

汽车实用英语

Instrument Cluster

Instrument cluster is mounted on the dashboard of vehicles, which can inform the driver of the operation of the engine of the vehicle（shown as Figure10-2）.

gauge [geidʒ] n.测量仪表，直径，规格；
　　　　　　vt.估计，计量
optimum ['ɔptiməm]
　　　　adj.最合适的，最优的，最佳的
malfunction [mæl'fʌŋkʃən]
　　　　　　n.故障，障碍
moderately ['mɔdərətli]
　　　　　adv.适度地，有节制地

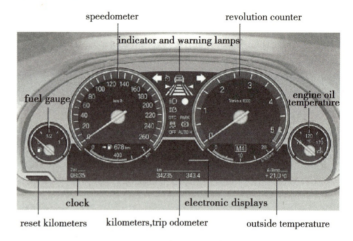

Figure 10-2　Instrument cluster

CBS Indicator and Warning Light

Newer BMW models feature a technology at the forefront of service innovation called Condition Based Servicing（CBS）, which ensures your BMW only receives attention when it needs it, saving time and money. [2]CBS sensors monitor the condition of parts such as spark plugs, filters, and brake pads as well as all operating fluids. A microchip in your remote control key stores the data, which our BMW Approved Technicians download via a Key Reader. We use Genuine BMW Parts to restore your BMW to optimum condition. The following is to check indicator and warning lights on instrument cluster（shown as　Table 10-1）.[3]

Check indicator and warning lights on instrument cluster Table 10-1

Variable indicator lamp	Check Control message	Clarification
	Active steering! Steer cautiously	Active steering fault. Steering behaviour altered. Steering wheel may be at an angle. Possible to continue the journey. Steer with care. Have the problem checked by the nearest BMW Service.
	EPS inoperative	EPS is inoperative. Have the problem checked by the nearest BMW Service.
	Brake light control failed!	Brake light failed. Have the problem checked by the nearest BMW Service.
	Oil level sensor malfunction!	Oil level sensor malfunction! Have the problem checked by BMW Service as soon as possible.
	Increased battery discharge!	High rate of battery discharge with engine stationary. It may not be possible to restart engine. Switch off unnecessary electric loads. Have the problem checked by BMW Service.
	Battery monitoring failed!	Battery charge status failed. Have the problem checked by BMW Service.
	Fuel pump fault! Drive moderately	Fuel pump. Fuel pump fault. Engine may stall. Possible reduction in engine power. Drive moderately! Have the problem checked by the nearest BMW Service.
	Battery not charged!	Alternator malfunction. Battery is no longer charged. Switch off unnecessary electric loads. Have checked by nearest BMW Service.
	Engine problem! Drive carefully	Engine problem. Increased engine load can damage catalytic converter. Drive at low engine load. Have checked by nearest BMW Service.
	ELV blocked! Move steering wheel	The "electric steering lock" ELV blocks the engine start function. Move steering wheel so that engine can be started.
	Engine problem! Loss of power	Engine problem. Full engine power no longer available. Drive carefully. Have the problem checked by the nearest BMW Service.

Continue

Variable indicator lamp	Check Control message	Clarification
	Engine oil pressure! Stop carefully	Engine oil pressure too low. Engine damage possible. Turn off engine. Not possible to continue journey. Contact the nearest BMW Service.
	Engine overheating! Stop carefully	Engine overheating. Turn off engine and allow to cool down. Do not open bonnet, danger of scalding. Risk of scalding! Contact the nearest BMW Service.
	Brakes too hot! Allow to cool down	Brakes too hot. Critical temperature as the result of high permanent load. Danger of reduced braking effect! Allow brakes to cool down. Stop if necessary.
	HDC currently not available!	HDC not available. Automatic brake intervention deactivated for safety reasons as brakes are overheated. Shift down gear and drive carefully to reduce temperature.
	HDC active!	HDC is activated.
	HDC deactivated!	HDC deactivated. Hill Descent Control HDC is deactivated at speed above 60 km/h. Reactivation possible at speed below 35 km/h.
	No HDC control! Drive slower	HDC not possible! Control range ends at 35km/h. Reduce speed correspondingly in order to use HDC.
	Tyre failure!	Tyre failure. Stop carefully. Refer to Owner's Handbook for wheel change procedure. Run flat tyres: Possible to continue driving at max speed of 80km/h for limited distance, see Owner's Handbook. Have tyres checked by the nearest BMW Service.
	Outside temperature	If the display drops to +3° C, the warning lamp lights up. A message appears on the control display. There is an increased danger of ice.

bonnet ['bɒnit]　　　　　　　　n.圆帽，扁平软帽
scalding ['skɔːldiŋ]　　　　　　adj.滚烫的
intervention [ˌɪntəˈvenʃən]
　　　　　　　　　　　　n.介入，干涉，干预
tyre ['taɪə]　　　　　　　　　　n.轮胎

How to Read the Wiring Diagram

　　The following wiring diagram is for Lexus IS200/300, the system shown here is an example only（shown as Figure 10-3）. It is different to the actual circuit shown in the wiring diagram section.

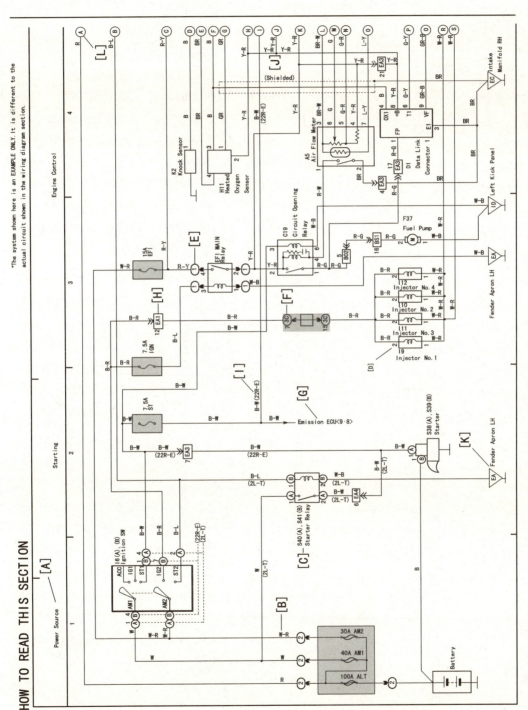

Figure 10-3 Engine control system wiring diagram

specification [,spesifi'keiʃən]
n.[pl.]技术规范，技术参数

In order to better use maintenance manuals, we have to learn how to read the wiring diagram. [4]

[A]: System Title

[B]: Indicates the wiring colour

Wire colours are indicated by an alphabetical code.

B=Black   W=White   BR=Brown
L=Blue   V=Violet   SB=Sky Blue
R=Red   G=Green   LG=Light Green
P=Pink   Y=Yellow
GR=Gray   O=Orange

The first letter indicates the basic wire colour and the second letter indicates the colour of the stripe.

Example: L-Y（shown as Figure 10-4）

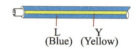

Figure 10-4　Wiring colour

[C]: The position of the parts is the same as shown in the wiring diagram and wire routing.

[D]: Indicates the pin number of the connector.

The numbering system is different for female and male connectors.（shown as Figure 10-5）

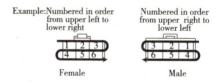

Figure 10-5　Pin number of the connector

The numbering system is different for female and male connectors.

[E]: Indicates a Relay Block. No shading is used and only the Relay Block No. is shown to distinguish it from the J/B. [5]

Example: ①Indicates Relay Block No.1

[F]: Junction Block（The number in the circle is the J/B No. and the connector code is shown beside it). Junction Blocks are shaded to clearly separate them from other parts.

Example:  3C indicates that it is inside Junction Block No.3

[G]: Indicates related system.

[H]: Indicates the wiring harness and wiring harness connector.

The wiring harness with male terminal is shown with arrows ⌵ (shown as Figure 10-6).

Outside numerals are pin numbers.

[I]: ( ) is used to indicate different wiring and connector, etc. When the vehicle model, engine type, or specification is different.

[J]: Indicates a shielded cable. (shown as Figure 10-7)

[K]: Indicates and located on ground point.

[L]: The same code occurring on the next page indicates that the wire harness is continuous.

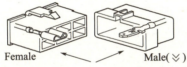

Figure 10-6 Wiring harness with male/female terminal

Figure 10-7 Shielded cable

HINT: Junction connector in this manual includes a short terminal which is connected to a number of wire harnesses. Always perform inspection with the short terminal installed. (When installing the wire harnesses, the harnesses can be connected to any position within the short terminal grouping. Accordingly, in other vehicles, the same position in the short terminal may be connected to a wire harness from a different part.)

Wire harness sharing the same short terminal grouping has the same colour.

ABBREVIATIONS

The following abbreviations are used in this manual. (shown as Table 10-2)

Relay Locations

Relay is an electronic control device often used in automatic control circuit. It is actually using less current to control a larger current "automatic switch." Therefore, the circuit automatically adjusts the play, security, conversion circuit and so on. The following describes the location of engine compartment relay, instrument cluster relay and body relay.

Abbreviations in the manual   Table 10-2

A/C	=	Air Conditioner
A/T	=	Automatic Transmission
ABS	=	Anti-Lock Brake System
ACIS	=	Acoustic Control induction System
BA	=	Brake Assist
COMB.	=	Combination
DLC3	=	Data Link Connector 3
ECT	=	Electronic Control Transmission
ECU	=	Electronic Control Unit
EFI	=	Electronic Fuel Injection
ESA	=	Electronic Spark Advance
ETCS-i	=	Electronic Throttle Control System-intelligent
EVAP	=	Evaporative Emission
FFC	=	Flexible Flat Circuit
HID	=	High Intensity Discharge
IC	=	Integrated Circuit
J/B	=	Junction Block
LED	=	Light Emitting Diode
LH	=	Left-Hand
LHD	=	Left-Hand Drive
M/T	=	Manual Transmission
MPX	=	Multiplex
O/D	=	Overdrive
R/B	=	Relay Block
RH	=	Right-Hand
RHD	=	Right-Hand Drive
S/D	=	Sedan Type
SRS	=	Supplemental Restraint System
SW	=	Switch
TEMP.	=	Temperature
TRC	=	Traction Control
VSC	=	Vehicle Stability Control
VSV	=	Vacuum Switching Valve
W/G	=	Wagon Type
W/	=	With
W/O	=	Without

Engine Compartment Relays (shown as Figure 10-8)

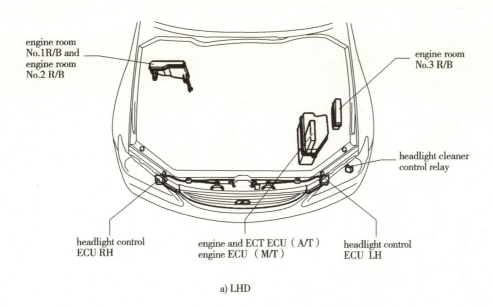

a) LHD

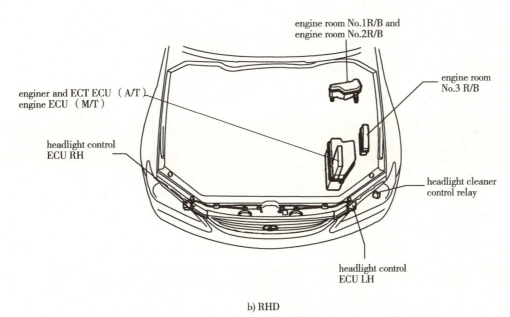

b) RHD

Figure 10-8　Location of engine compartment relays

Instrument Panel Relays (shown as Figure10-9)

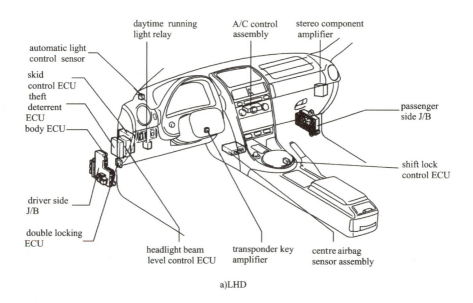

a) LHD

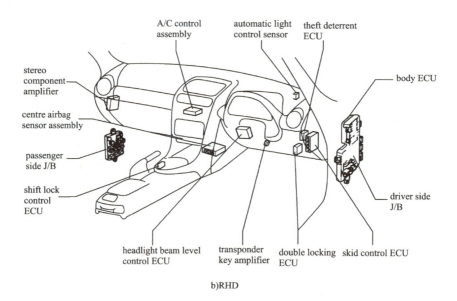

b) RHD

Figure10-9　Location of instrument panel relays

Body Relays (shown as Figure 10-10)

Word List

transponder [træn'spɔndə]　　n.转发器
amplifier ['æmplifaiə]　　n.放大器,扩音机

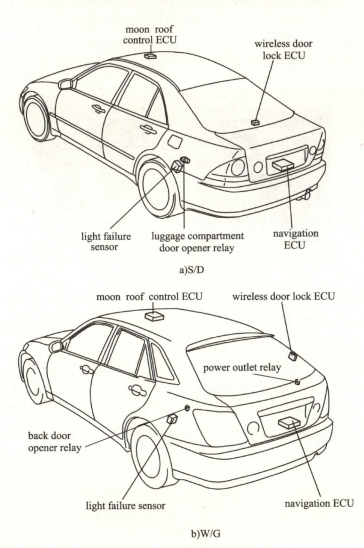

Figure 10-10　Location of body relays

Fuse Locations

Fuses are fitted to circuits to provide protection for both the circuit and for the component. Most of the fuses in a vehicle are contained in a fuse block located inside the vehicle or in the engine compartment, but separate line fuses are sometimes used for auxiliary components.

Fuses are rated according to their current-carrying capacity, such as 10 amps and 15 amps. Fuses range from 5 amps, used for radios, up to 60 amps, used for air conditioning or heater fans.

Three different types of fuses and a line-type fuse holder are shown in Figure 10-11. The cartridge-type fuse has its element in a small glass tube with metal contacts on each end. The ceramic type is similar, but uses a ceramic carrier with a metal strip, while the blade type of fuse has its element connected between two blades. This type of fuse is commonly used.

Figure10-11　Types of fuses

Handy hint : Fuses are marked with their rating and also colour coded for ease of identification. Any fuse that is replaced must have the same amps rating as the original.

Figure10-12 shows how the fuses and relays can be centralised for a vehicle. There are two blocks of these: a power distribution box in the engine compartment and an interior fuse panel beneath the instrument panel.

The location of the fuses and relays, as shown, is for a particular vehicle. They could be in different places in other vehicles, although below the instrument panel is a common location.

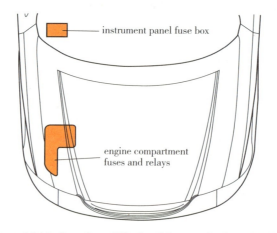

Figure 10-12　Location of blocks of fuses and relays (FORD)

Power Distribution Box

The power distribution box in the engine compartment in Figure 10-13 has eleven relays and ten fuses. The ratings of the fuses range from 5 amps to 60 amps, although there is a main fuse that is rated at 120 amps. The box also contains a circuit breaker for the headlamps which is rated at 30 amps.

The various circuits that the fuses protect are identified in the illustration. These are for components within the engine compartment or towards the front of the vehicle. They include the cooling fan, fuel pump, headlamps and horn.

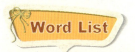

cartridge ['kɑ:tridʒ]　　　　n. 管壳,盒
ceramic [si'ræmik]　adj. 陶瓷的,陶器的;
　　　　　　　　　　　　n. 陶瓷,陶瓷制品
strip [strip]　　　　　　　　n. 带；条状
blade [bleid]　　n. 叶片,刀片，刀锋,剑

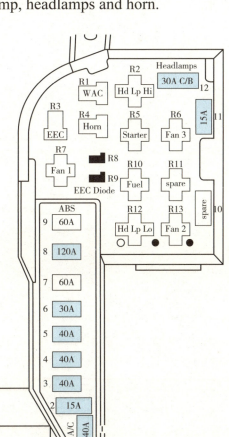

Figure 10-13　Contents of a power distribution box in the engine compartment (FORD)

The contents of a power distribution box in other brand engine compartment are different (shown as Figure 10-14).

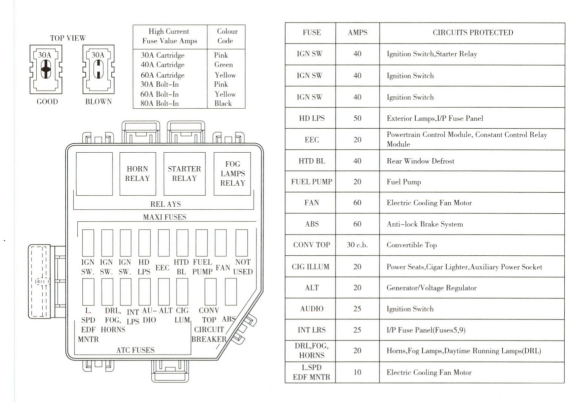

Figure 10-14 Contents of a power distribution box in the another engine compartment

Interior Fuse Panel

The interior fuse panel shown in Figure 10-15 is mounted below the instrument panel. It has five relays and over twenty fuses. The ratings of the fuses range from 5 amps to 30 amps. There is also a 30 amp circuit breaker for the power windows.

The fuses and relays in this panel are associated with components that are mostly inside the vehicle or towards the rear of the vehicle. These fuses are in the circuits for the windscreen wiper, reversing lamps, interior blower motor, turn signals and door locks and for other components.

There are relays on the panel for the air conditioning, the tail lamps and other components.

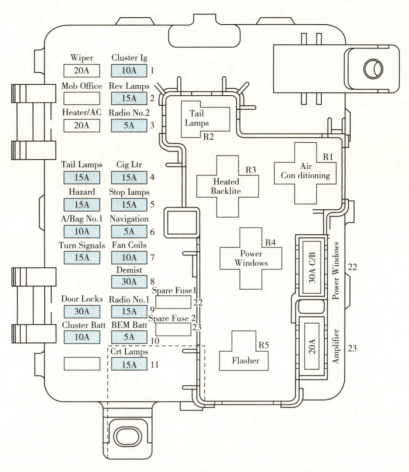

Figure 10-15 Interior block of fuses and relays FORD

Some common abbreviations fuse shown as table 10-3.

Common abbreviations fuse　　　　　　　　　　　　　　　Table 10-3

英　文　名	中　文　名	英　文　名	中　文　名
MIR DEFG	车外后视镜除雾器	RR DEFG	后除雾继电器
T/SIG	驻车/空挡位置以及倒车灯开关	PWRLK	门锁继电器
WIPER	刮水器/清洗器开关	HDLTS	前照灯继电器，日行灯模块
MEM SEAT	座椅调节开关存储模块	H/LAMP HILH	左远光灯
CCM IGN3	遥控门锁接收器以及防盗模块	H/LAMP HIRH	右远光灯
A/C COMP	空调压缩机继电器	H/LAMP LOLH	左近光灯
HORN	喇叭继电器	H/LAMP LORH	右近光灯
HAZARD LTS	危险警告灯闪烁器	ROOM LAMP	阅读灯
PWR MIR	外后视镜	FOG LAMP	雾灯
CORNR LTS	组合开关/音响控制	METET LAMP	仪表灯
I/P DIM LTS	前照灯开关	TURN SIGNAL	转向信号灯
STOP LTS	制动灯开关	POWER WINDOW	电动车窗
TAIL LTS	尾灯和牌照灯	IGN SW	点火开关

Common Faults Read From VAG 1552 or PIWIS(shown as table 10-4).

Common faults read　　　　　　　　　Table 10-4

英　文　显　示	中　文　含　义
No signal	没有信号
Control unit defective	控制单元损坏
Short to positive	对正极短路
Short circuit to earth	对搭铁短路
Electrical fault in circuit	电路中电气故障
Fuel cut-off valve -N109 Malfunction	燃料切断阀N109故障
Engine control unit blocked	封锁发动机控制单元
Voltage too low	电压太低
Load switch-off	用电设备关闭
No communication with seat control unit, driver	与驾驶员侧座椅控制单元无通信
No communication with seat control unit, front passenger	与前排乘客侧座椅控制单元无通信
No communication with rear lid control unit	与后盖控制单元无通信
No communication with instrument cluster	与组合仪表无通信
No communication with A/C control unit	与空调控制单元无通信
Check PSM control unit fault memory content(No fault symptom)	检查PSM控制单元故障记忆内容（无故障现象）
No communication with air conditioner regulator	与空调调节器无通信
Elec. steering lock motor, power supply	电子转向锁电动机，电源
EI. Steering lock enable line, short circuit to ground	电子转向锁启用线路，对搭铁短路
1 to 2 wheel electronics units are not detected	未检测到1到2轮的电子单元
Wheel electronics rear left, no reception	左后轮电子单元不接收信号
Fuel high pressure quantity (below Minimum Threshold)	燃油高压值（低于极限值）
Fuel pressure/quantity too low at start(Limit valve exceeded)	起动时燃油压力/值过低（超过极限值）

Proper Names

   1.gentleman function　　　　　　　　　绅士功能

   2.roller sunblind　　　　　　　　　　　遮阳卷帘

   3.lane departure warning　　　　　　　车道变换警告

   4.lane deviation warning　　　　　　　车道偏离警告

   5.Head–Up Display　　　　　　　　　平视显示器

   6.low–beam–dipped–headlights　　　近光灯

   7.onboard computer　　　　　　　　　车载电脑

   8.calling up the speed　　　　　　　　调出速度

   9.instrument cluster　　　　　　　　　组合仪表板

   10.entertainment source　　　　　　　视听设备

11. rain sensor 雨量传感器
12. opening luggage compartment lid 打开行李舱盖
13. revolution counter 转速表
14. EPS 电子助力转向
15. wiring diagram 电路图
16. maintenance manual 维修手册
17. female and male connectors 插座和插头
18. relay block 继电器座
19. air conditioner 空调
20. acoustic control induction system 声控感应系统
21. evaporative emission 蒸发排放
22. vehicle stability control 车辆稳定控制
23. stereo component amplifier 立体声放大组件
24. theft deterrent ECU 防盗电控单元
25. cluster ig 点火线束
26. mob office 手机办公
27. rev lamps 转向灯
28. heater/AC 加热器/空调
29. tail lamps 尾灯
30. hazard 风险
31. a/bag 安全气囊
32. navigation 导航
33. spare 备用
34. fan coil 风扇线圈
35. demist 除雾
36. radio 收音机

Notes

[1] It also contains useful information which will help you to uphold both the car's operating safety and its full resale value.

翻译：此外，您还会得到对本车行驶安全性及汽车最佳保值非常有用的信息。

[2] Newer BMW models feature a technology at the forefront of service innovation called Condition Based Servicing（CBS）, which ensures your BMW

only receives attention when it needs it, saving time and money.

翻译：新宝马车型的特点是运用了一项叫基于状态服务（CBS）的最前沿的服务创新技术，以确保您的宝马车只在需要时接受服务，节约了时间和金钱。

[3] The following is to check indicator and warning lights on instrument cluster (shown as Table 10-1).

翻译：随后是检查仪表板上的指示和警告灯（见表10-1）。

[4] In order to better use maintenance manuals, we have to learn how to read the wiring diagram.

翻译：为了更好地使用维护手册，我们必须学会如何阅读电路图。

[5] Indicates a Relay Block. No shading is used and only the Relay Block No. is shown to distinguish it from the J/B.

翻译：表示继电器座。不要使用阴影，仅标出继电器编号，以便与接线盒区分开。

Exercises

1. Choose the best answer from the following choices according to the text.

 1）The better you are ____ with your car, the easer you will find it is to handle.

　　A. know　　B. known　　C. acquainted　　D. acquainting

 2）It contains important notes on how to operate the car, enabling you to ____ maximum benefit from the technical advantages of your BMW.

　　A. get　　B. derive　　C. receive　　D. oppose

 3）Automatic brake intervention deactivated for safety reasons as brakes are ____.

　　A. heated　　B. boiled　　C. cooled　　D. overheated

 4）Junction Blocks are shaded to clearly separate them ____ other parts.

　　A. from　　B. with　　C. out　　D. in

2. Translate the following words or phrases into Chinese.

 1）gentleman function　　2）lane departure warning　　3）indicator

 4）onboard computer　　5）rain sensor　　6）revolution counter

 7）wiring diagram　　8）air conditioner　　9）malfunction

3. Translate the following words or phrases into English.

 1）遮阳卷帘　　2）车道偏离警告　　3）近光灯

 4）车载电脑　　5）组合仪表板　　6）电路图

 7）继电器座　　8）雨量传感器　　9）防盗电控单元

4. Translate the following sentences into Chinese.

1）Junction Blocks are shaded to clearly separate them from other parts.

2）The wiring harness with male terminal is shown with arrows（∨）.

3）Junction connector in this manual includes a short terminal which is connected to a number of wire harnesses.

4）Wire harness sharing the same short terminal grouping has the same color.

5. Translate the words or phrases in the following figure into Chinese.

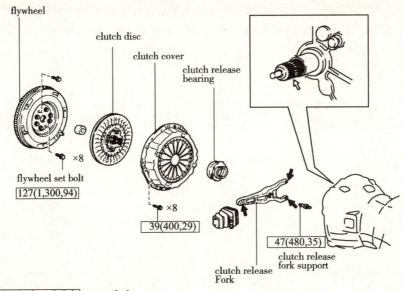

Practical Reading　Idle Control System rpm Lower than Expected

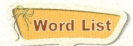

detect [di'tekt]
　　　　　vt.察觉，发现；查明，侦查出
consecutive [kən'sekjutiv]
　　　　　adj.连续的，连贯的
description [dis'kripʃən]
　　　　　n.描写，形容；种类，性质
symptom ['simptəm]　n.症状，征候，征兆
stall [stɔ:l]　n.熄火；v.（使）熄火，拖延
clog [klɔg]　　　　　vt.塞满，阻塞

DTC Detecting Condition

★Two consecutive driving cycles with fault

★GENERAL DESCRIPTION <Ref. to GD（H4SO）-141, DTC P0506 IDLE CONTROL SYSTEM RPM LOWER THAN EXPECTED, Diagnostic Trouble Code（DTC）Detecting Criteria.>

Trouble Symptom

★ Engine is difficult to start.

★ Engine does not start.

★ Erroneous idling.

★ Engine stalls.

Caution

After repair or replacement of faulty parts, conduct Clear Memory Mode <Ref. to EN（H4SO）（diag）-46, OPERATION, Clear Memory Mode.> and Inspection Mode <Ref. to EN（H4SO）（diag）-36, PROCEDURE, Inspection Mode.>.Table 10-5 shows the diagnostic Process.

Diagnostic Process   Table 10-5

Step	Check	Yes	No
1.Check any other DTC on display.	Is any other DTC displayed?	Inspect the relevant DTC using "List of Diagnostic Trouble Code（DTC）". NOTE: In this case, it is not necessary to inspect DTC P0506.	Go to step 2.
2.Check air cleaner element. 1）Turn the ignition switch to OFF. 2）Check air cleaner element.	Is there excessive clogging on air cleaner element?[1]	Replace the air cleaner element.	Go to step 3.
3.Check electronic throttle control. 1）Turn the ignition switch to OFF. 2）Remove the electronic throttle control. 3）Check the electronic throttle control.	Are there foreign particles in electronic throttle control?	Remove the foreign particles from electronic throttle control.[2]	Perform the diagnosis of DTC P2101（Throttle Actuator control Motor Circuit Range/Performance）

Proper Names

1. memory mode　　　　　　　　　　　　内存模式
2. electronic throttle control　　　　　　　电子节气门控制

Notes

[1] Is there excessive clogging on air cleaner element?
翻译：空气滤清器的滤芯是否过度堵塞？

[2] Remove the foreign particles from electronic throttle control.
翻译：清除电子节气门控制系统上的外来颗粒。

 学习资料

[1] http://carpdf.net.
[2] http://www.ebookee.net/Complete-Car-Care-Manual-PDF-864701.html.
[3] http://wenku.baidu.com/view/dd68d81fc5da50e2524d7f45.html.

参考答案

项 目 1

1. Choose the best answer from the following choices according to the text.

   1）A 2）B 3）C 4）A

2. Translate the following words or phrases into Chinese.

   1）进气行程 2）正时齿轮 3）水泵
   4）连杆 5）燃烧室 6）曲柄销
   7）下止点 8）汽缸盖 9）风扇皮带轮

3. Translate the following words or phrases into English.

   1）cylinder block 2）solar cell 3）crankcase
   4）oil pan 5）timing belt 6）piston ring
   7）ignition distributor 8）spark plug 9）main bearing journal

4. Translate the following sentences into Chinese.

   1）这些包括起动系统、电源系统、冷却系统、点火系统、润滑系统、燃油系统和排气系统。

   2）这四个行程分别是进气行程、压缩行程、做功行程和排气行程。

   3）动力通过连杆传递到曲柄销，从而导致曲轴旋转。

5. Translate the words or phrases in the following figure into Chinese.

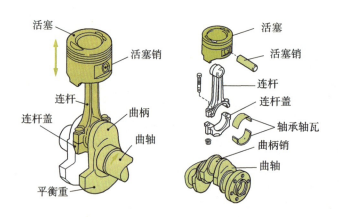

项 目 2

1.Choose the best answer from the following choices according to the text.

　　1）D　　　　　2）B　　　　　3）C　　　　　4）B

2.Translate the following words or phrases into Chinese.

　　1）电子燃油喷射　　　2）活性炭罐　　　　3）单点燃油喷射

　　4）燃油滤清器　　　　5）发动机起动性　　6）发动机舱

　　7）压力调节器　　　　8）燃油回油管　　　9）空气流量计

3. Translate the following words or phrases into English.

　　1）fuel system　　　　　　2）fuel filter　　　　　　3）air flow meter

　　4）electronic fuel injection　5）multipoint fuel injection　6）cold start injector

　　7）throttle body injection　　8）air induction system　　9）fuel supply line

4. Translate the following sentences into Chinese.

　　1）燃油供给系的作用是给发动机提供可燃的空气燃油混合物。

　　2）空气进气系统的作用是过滤进入发动机空气中的杂质，计量进气量，并测量空气温度。

　　3）每一个汽缸都有单独的喷油器，可以将燃油直接喷到进气门处。

5. Translate the words or phrases in the following figure into Chinese.

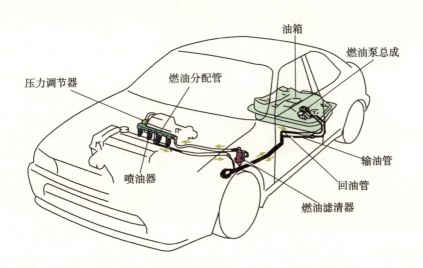

项 目 3

1. Choose the best answer from the following choices according to the text.

  1）B   2）C   3）A

2. Translate the following words or phrases into Chinese.

  1）冷却系   2）节温器   3）散热器盖

  4）散热器芯   5）润滑系   6）曲轴箱通风

  7）黏度指数改进剂 8）漆膜   9）油泥

3. Translate the following words or phrases into English.

  1）water pump   2）anti-freeze coolant   3）water-cooled engine

  4）lubricating system 5）lubricant   6）oxidation inhibitor

  7）engine deposit   8）oil filter   9）metal-to-metal contact

4. Translate the following sentences into Chinese.

  1）发动机内摩擦过大意味着其快速损坏。

  2）为减小锈蚀的生成，商用防冻剂内含有防锈剂。

5. Translate the words or phrases in the following figure into Chinese.

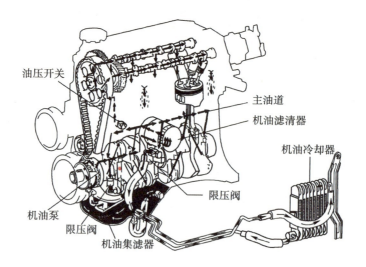

项 目 4

1.Choose the best answer from the following choices according to the text.

　　1）D　　　　2）C　　　　3）B　　　　4）B　　　　5）C

2.Translate the following words or phrases into Chinese.

　　1）转向摇臂　　　2）自动变速器　　　3）行星齿轮系

　　4）底盘　　　　　5）万向节　　　　　6）转向系

　　7）制动系　　　　8）行车制动系　　　9）驻车制动系

3. Translate the following words or phrases into English.

　　1）power train　　2）manual transmission　　3）differential

　　4）rear-wheel drive　5）steering wheel　　　　6）leaf spring

　　7）brake shoe　　　8）suspension system　　　9）brake pedal

4. Translate the following sentences into Chinese.

　　1）万向节用于将传动轴与变速器输出轴连接。

　　2）货车转向系有人力的，也有助力的。助力转向单元（装置）使用辅助单元，使用液压或气动装置来使转向变得轻便。

　　3）转向盘直径越大，则同样的转向力可产生的转向力矩越大。

5. Translate the words or phrases in the following figure into Chinese.

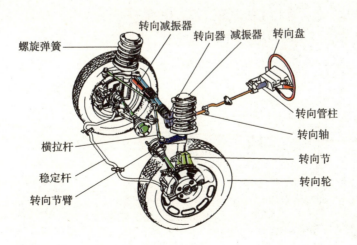

项 目 5

1. Choose the best answer from the following choices according to the text.

   1）A 2）B 3）D 4）B 5）A

2. Translate the following words or phrases into Chinese.

   1）电子点火系统 2）发动机控制单元 3）初级电流
   4）交流发电机 5）过度转向 6）充电系统
   7）继电器 8）起动机 9）柱塞

3. Translate the following words or phrases into English.

   1）spark plug 2）ignition switch 3）ignition control unit
   4）starter 5）battery 6）voltage regulator
   7）circuit 8）direct current 9）drive belt
   10）ESP 11）ECU 12）active safety systems

4. Translate the following sentences into Chinese.

   1）充电系统的作用是为蓄电池充电提供电能，以及为车上的电气元件与系统提供电能。

   2）内燃机在依靠自身产生的能量运转之前必须先旋转起来。

   3）汽车蓄电池不能为汽车电气设备提供长时间的供电。（因此）每辆汽车都必须装备一种装置来替代蓄电池为汽车用电设备提供电能。

   4）如果防抱死制动系统的控制单元探测到一个或者多个车轮趋于抱死，那么它就会在几毫秒内介入制动控制，调整每个车轮的制动压力。

5. Translate the words or phrases in the following figure into Chinese.

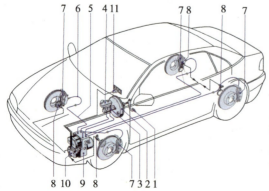

1-制动踏板；2-制动伺服单元；3-主缸；4-制动液储液罐；5-制动管路；6-制动软管；7-盘式制动器；8-车轮轮速传感器；9-液压调节器；10-ABS控制单元；11-ABS警告灯

项 目 6

1.Choose the best answer from the following choices according to the text.

　　1）B　　　　2）C　　　　3）B　　　　4）B　　　　5）A

2.Translate the following words or phrases into Chinese.

　　1）安全气囊　　　　2）压缩机　　　　3）电动坐椅

　　4）六向电动坐椅　　5）储液罐　　　　6）防盗系统

　　7）转向灯　　　　　8）安全带　　　　9）尾灯

3.Translate the following words or phrases into English.

　　1）condenser　　　　　　　2）air bag　　　　　　　　3）compressor

　　4）licence plate　　　　　　5）evaporator　　　　　　6）refrigerant

　　7）thermal expansion valve　8）central locking system　9）reversing lamps

4. Translate the following sentences into Chinese.

　　1）车辆后部的灯包括：制动灯（红色灯罩）、尾灯（红色灯罩）、倒车灯（白色灯罩）和转向灯（琥珀色灯罩）。除了这些，还有号牌（牌照）灯。

　　2）锁定或开启车门，都可以通过遥控来实现，这和电视机的遥控操作是一样的。

　　3）在大多数情况下，冷凝器与汽车上的散热器的外观很相似，而且它们有非常相似的功能。

5.Translate the words or phrases in the following figure into Chinese.

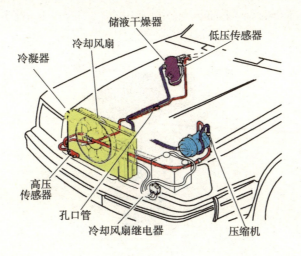

项 目 7

1. Choose the best answer from the following choices according to the text.

   1）B 2）A 3）D 4）C

2. Translate the following words or phrases into Chinese.

   1）二氧化碳 2）压缩空气 3）电动机，起动机
   4）燃料电池汽车 5）油电混合汽车 6）有害排放
   7）锂离子电池 8）串联混合 9）太阳能汽车

3. Translate the following words or phrases into English.

   1）parallel hybrid 2）electric car 3）photovoltaic cell
   4）air powered vehicle 5）gasoline engine 6）fuel cell stack
   7）solar panel 8）carbon-fiber 9）greenhouse gas

4. Translate the following sentences into Chinese.

   1）光伏电池由半导体材料制成，例如硅以及铟、镓和氮的合金。

   2）一辆电动汽车是一辆由充电电池提供能量，由电动机驱动的汽车。

   3）燃料电池汽车具有显著减少我们对于国外石油的依赖，并且有效降低造成气候变化的有害排放的潜力。

   4）空气压缩汽车的能量来源通常是电能，因此，它对环境的总体影响取决于电能来源的清洁程度。

5. Translate the words or phrases in the following figure into Chinese.

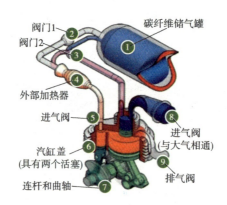

项 目 8

1. Choose the best answer from the following choices according to the text.

   1）B 　　2）D 　　3）A 　　4）C

2. Translate the following words or phrases into Chinese.

   1）微型计算机　　2）技师　　3）速度表

   4）主销内倾角　　5）车轮外倾角　　6）透明度测试仪

   7）燃油消耗率　　8）泄漏检测仪　　9）动力吸收单元

3. Translate the following words or phrases into English.

   1）diesel smoke meter　　　　2）chassis dynamometer

   3）engine test bed　　　　　　4）4-wheel alignment gauge

   5）engine analyzer　　　　　　6）slid-slip tester

   7）fifth wheel sensor　　　　　8）single board computer

   9）wheel dynamic balancer

4. Translate the following sentences into Chinese.

   1）红外线分析仪是一种用来测量汽车尾气中HC和CO含量的设备。

   2）这种仪器用来测试汽车前轮的动力学部位。

   3）这是一台带有微型计算机的扭矩测量仪，用于测量发动机、电动机和变速器的扭矩、转速和功率。

   4）这台仪器用于测量和校正连杆的弯曲和扭转变形的。

5. Translate the words or phrases in the following figure into Chinese.

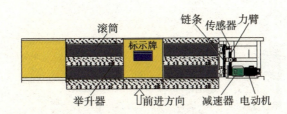

项 目 9

1.Choose the best answer from the following choices according to the text.

　　1）B　　　　　　2）A　　　　　　3）D　　　　　　4）C

2.Translate the following words or phrases into Chinese.

　　1）反接　　　　　　　　　　　　2）扁平插座

　　3）发动机电控　　　　　　　　　4）柴油泵电子控制系统

　　5）制动系电子控制系统　　　　　6）安全气囊

　　7）故障存储器　　　　　　　　　8）车轮阻尼电子控制系统

　　9）空调/暖风电子控制系统

3.Translate the following words or phrases into English.

　　1）diagnostic tester　　2）fault memory　　　　　　3）negative electrode

　　4）operating mode　　　5）flat-contact socket　　　6）gearbox electronics

　　7）airbag　　　　　　　8）combination instrument　9）electronic roof control

4. Translate the following sentences into Chinese.

　　1）当有新的车型上市，测试仪内的软件则必须升级。因此，必须更换程序卡。

　　2）只有当电源被切断后，或者说，测试电源没有接到汽车上时才可以拆下或插上程序卡。

　　3）如果自检测完成后没有故障产生，则不再需要旧程序卡。

　　4）如果你现在按下键Q，测试仪将建立与控制单元的数据联系。

5.Translate the words or phrases in the following figure into Chinese.

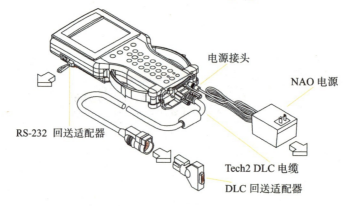

项 目 10

1. Choose the best answer from the following choices according to the text.
   1）C 2）B 3）D 4）A

2. Translate the following words or phrases into Chinese.
   1）绅士功能 2）车道变换警告 3）指示物
   4）车载电脑 5）雨量传感器 6）转速表
   7）线路图 8）空调 9）故障

3. Translate the following words or phrases into English.
   1）roller sunblind 2）lane deviation warning
   3）low-beam-dipped-headlights 4）onboard computer
   5）instrument cluster 6）wiring diagram
   7）relay block 8）rain sensor
   9）theft deterrent ECU

4. Translate the following sentences into Chinese.
   1）给接线盒加涂阴影以清楚地区别于其他零件。
   2）带插头的线束用箭头⌵来表示。
   3）本手册中的转接连接器包含一个与许多线束相连接的短接线柱。
   4）共用同一个端子的线束，颜色相同。

5. Translate the words or phrases in the following figure into Chinese.

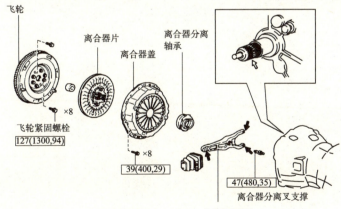